THE
LITTLE
BOOK
OF
THE BLACK
COUNTRY

MICHAEL PEARSON

First published 2013

The History Press
The Mill, Brimscombe Port
Stroud, Gloucestershire, GL5 2QG
www.thehistorypress.co.uk

British Library Cataloguing in Publication Data.
A catalogue record for this book is available from the British Library.

ISBN 978 0 7524 8783 0

Typesetting and origination by The History Press
Printed in Great Britain

CONTENTS

CONTENTS

INTRODUCTION

I hope this 'little' book will hit the spot in your thirst for knowledge. I have tried to delve into the deeper corners of research material for those more obscure facts, and have learnt much myself about some of the funnier, odder or downright sinister bits of Black Country history. You, the reader, will probably read some and think 'I know that', but hopefully there will be much more you will not have heard or read before.

One difficulty I always have when writing about the Black Country is balance; with two former counties, four boroughs, nine or ten substantial towns and innumerable smaller settlements, I don't want to leave anyone out. But it does make writing a bit more of a puzzle.

As always, there are people I want to thank for their help. Firstly my wife, for putting up with papers and books being strewn around the house while I was gathering my research material, and my step-daughter Rachael, who drew some of the images contained here. Also Doctor Michael Hall for his assistance on Francis Brett Young, and finally the Black Country Society for providing a wealth of written material over a forty-six year period, which provides me with so many avenues for my research

I hope this book provides enjoyment and some enlightenment about this great region of ours.

Michael Pearson, 2013

THE BLACK COUNTRY SOCIETY

This voluntary society of some 1,800 members worldwide is associated with the British Association for Local History (BALH). It was founded in 1967 as a reaction to the late 1950s/early 1960s trend of amalgamating local authorities and other bodies into larger units. In the Midlands, this swept away the area's industrial heritage in the process.

The general aim of the society is to create interest in the past, present and future of the Black Country. It campaigned for the establishment of an industrial museum, and in 1975 the Black Country Museum was established on twenty-six acres of derelict land adjoining Dudley Castle grounds. This has been developed into an award-winning museum, attracting over 250,000 annually.

All members receive a copy of the quarterly magazine, *The Blackcountryman*, over 180 of which have been published. In these magazines are some 3,500 authoritative articles on all aspects of the Black Country, by historians, teachers, researchers, students, subject experts and ordinary folk with an extraordinary story to tell. The whole represents a unique resource about the area, a mine of information for students and researchers who frequently refer to it. 2,000 copies are printed and contributors do not receive payment for their articles.

W: www.blackcountrysociety.co.uk
E: editor@blackcountrysociety.co.uk
PO Box 71 Kingswinford DY6 9YN

1

BEFORE THE BLACK COUNTRY

DOMESDAY BOOK AND BEFORE

The very earliest inhabitants of Dudley were not humans, but a class of marine animals from which lobsters, crabs and shrimp evolved. Sometimes compared to the wood louse, they lived in shallow seas, grubbing about on the seabed looking for food.

I am describing a trilobite, the variety being *Calymene Blumenbachii*, better known as the Dudley Locust. They lived during the Silurian period (about 443 to 416 million years ago), and died out during the period when the coal swamps were being formed. The best specimens come from limestone excavations from the Industrial Revolution.

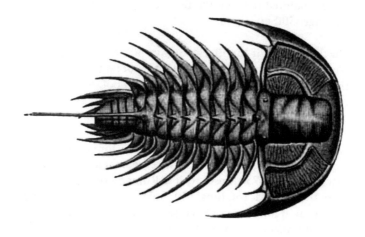

There were very early human residents at Sandwell. There is evidence of human inhabitation in the Sandwell Valley as early as 6000–4000 BC. Over 800 flint tools and debris have been found, dated to the later Mesolithic Period (about 10,000–5000 BC). This was when humans began their first steps in land management. It followed the retreat of the glaciers from the Pleistocene period, and man began to move north.

The first evidence of farming was also in Sandwell Valley from the Neolithic Period about 4000–2500 BC; tools to cut down trees and clear ground were found. The region continued to be inhabited through the Bronze Age (2500–500 BC) and Iron Age (500 BC–AD 43).

On the fringes of the Black Country at Streetly, remains of Neolithic Man and substantial numbers of flints were found in the 1950s in a field surrounding Bourne Pool. An excavation took place and it concluded that the land was used as a campsite and an early factory for making flint tools.

A number of Roman remains have been found around the region. At Rowley Regis a cracked earthenware pot was discovered in 1794, next to it a Roman coin. More coins were then found, totalling 120. Some years later the hoard disappeared and has not been seen since. Further finds were made at Cakemore near Halesowen and Hurst Hill at Sedgley.

As Roman influences receded, the Anglo-Saxons came onto the scene. Their influence can be seen in many of the place names in the Black Country. 'Ton' at the end of a town name is an Anglo-Saxon influence, and clearings on hill slopes for pasture were named 'leah', as seen in Warley, Dudley and Cradley.

The Celtic influence is also still present, in names such as Kinver and Pencricket Lane in Blackheath. It is thought that people whose roots lie firmly in the Black Country will have a mixture of Anglo-Saxon and Celtic DNA, probably with a bit of Roman and some coal dust.

Early religion in the Black Country was Christian, from the days when the Anglo-Saxons became Christian. St Chad's diocese was founded at Lichfield and covered the land that became the Black Country.

In the eighth century the martyrdom of St Kenelm took place on Clent Hills. The Mercian boy-prince Kenelm was put under the guardianship of a distinctly unsavoury character. He awoke from a puzzling nightmare and asked his nurse for interpretation. It involved a tree with Kenelm at the top of it. A band of men began chopping down the tree and then Kenelm grew wings and flew towards heaven. He was murdered a short time later.

The Pope sent emissaries to investigate the incident and discovered Kenelm's body beneath a hawthorn that had sprung up. Nearby, a clear water spring was found, thought to have healing properties. A shrine was built on the hillside which became a place for great pilgrimage; later a church was built under the patronage of Halesowen Abbey.

The Battle of Tettenhall took place in AD 910 in August. It is said that Edward the Elder, the Saxon King, supplied the army that defeated the Danes and halted their invasion of England. The army was probably led by Lord Aethelred II of Mercia and his wife Aethelfleda, 'Lady of the Mercians'.

The location of the battle is unclear. Aside from Tettenhall, other suggested sites have been Wednesfield, Stowheath or even Wombourne Common. It is alleged, in different accounts, that two or three Danish Kings were killed during the battle.

PLACES FROM DOMESDAY BOOK AND BEFORE

Darlaston	–	Deorlaf's Town / Derlavestone
Wolverhampton	–	Heantune (Hantone) AD 985
Tettenhall	–	Totehala (or Totenhale)
Wednesbury	–	Wadnesberie
Willenhall	–	Winehala
Tipton	–	Tibintone / Tibbington
Sedgley	–	Segleslei
Amblecote	–	Elmelecote
Halesowen	–	Hala
Warley	–	Werwelie
Dudley	–	Dudelei
Cradley	–	Cradelei
Pelsall	–	Peolshale
Smethwick	–	Smedewich

In 1086–87 King William ordered the Domesday Survey so data was collected on each parcel of land (or hide). A hundred hides made up a 'hundred'. Staffordshire was made up of five hundreds; two of them were Seisdon and Offlow, and these made up much of the northern part of the Black Country.

The rest, mainly the southern acres, were partly in Worcestershire and partly Shropshire (Halesowen was a detached part of Shropshire for a time).

Many names in the Domesday Book are unrecognisable from those acquired later, although some can be easily guessed, e.g. Wednesberie and Billestune. There are some significant errors: Walsall, Oldbury, Stourbridge and Darlaston have no mention; and Cippermore and Haswic have no modern day equivalent.

The survey shows that the King himself owned a considerable part of the South Staffordshire land. He had hunting rights from Pensnett to Kinver, and owned much of Bloxwich, Bilston and Willenhall. With ninety-six people, Wednesbury was the most populous place he held, compared to thirty-two in Birmingham and forty-six at West Bromwich.

Modern-day translations of the Domesday Survey are available to help decipher what was written in 1086/87; the information gives a fascinating insight into life in the rural midlands 500 years before the beginning of the Industrial Revolution.

R. pearson

In the twelfth and thirteenth centuries, three monastic priories were built in the Black Country. In 1130 the Benedictine Order built Sandwell Priory in the forest of West Bromwich, close to the 'Sanwell'. By 1526, when it was suppressed, it was already in a ruined condition.

Dudley Priory was founded in 1180 by the Cluniac Order, and was founded in the shadow of Dudley Castle. It was also dissolved in 1540, but its ruins remain today in Priory Park.

Halesowen Priory was the third Black Country monastery, founded in 1214 as a convent for the white canons of St Mary's. The boundaries of land owned by the Manor Abbey were marked by crosses as follows: Haden Cross at the foot of High Haden, Holy Cross at Clent, Lye Cross, and the fourth was at Rood End.

The significance of Halesowen Priory was said to be their relic. Enclosed in a jewelled shrine was the complete head of St Barbara, a Roman saint. Her head was cut off by her father 1,000 years previously because she was a Christian.

A report of Barbara's relics being located at St Michael's Golden-Domed Monastery in Kiev, cloud the claim for Halesowen. But no report I have found actually mentions the head of the saint being anywhere but at Halesowen.

On dissolution by Henry VIII, a farmhouse was built into Halesowen Priory ruins. It is still part of Manor Farm today and so not physically accessible to the public, but it is viewable from a public footpath.

2

SOME TOWN
AND PLACE FACTS

Stourbridge – Its present name came from 'bridge over the river Stour', but how did the river get its name? Duignan states that the early form of the name was 'Sture', the same as the other five rivers in England now called Stour. In the Subsidy Rolls of 1333 it was 'Sturbrugg' and later in 1375 it had evolved to 'Stourbrugge', 'Brugge' being an old form of the word bridge.

It is thought that Stourbridge town existed before Domesday, under the name 'Sture', which was mentioned in AD 781. Prior to the reign of Henry VI (1422–1453) Stourbridge was called 'Bedcote', an earlier name being 'Bettecote', meaning 'Betta's Cot'.

Dudley – Dudley Castle is described as towering up on a hill (now Castle Hill) and is named after English Saxon Dudo (or Dodo). The castle was built around AD 700 and is mentioned in the Domesday Book (AD 1086) as being owned by William Fitz Ansculph.

West Bromwich – West Bromwich was a country village in the reign of Edward I.

Nearby Wednesbury has a history dating back to Saxon times, named after the old Saxon Jove 'Woden'. A strong castle was built in AD 916 by Princess Ethelfreda, daughter of King Alfred (I wonder if she burned the cakes?) This was on the site now occupied by the parish church.

Cradley became a medieval manor and was linked to Hales Owen, then a detached part of Shropshire. Cradley stayed in

Worcestershire, but to avoid confusion with the 'other' Cradley in Worcestershire, it became known as Cradley Staffordshire.

In 1974 with the amalgamation and creation of the West Midlands, the name 'Cradley' disappeared from postal addresses and it became part of Halesowen.

Sedgley – The beacon at Sedgley is said by some to have been the site of Druidical sacrifice and worship.

Walsall – it is said that the town may have furnished the bits, stirrups and spurs of many knights in the Wars of the Roses (1421–1487).

In 1540 the antiquary Leland said: 'Waulleshall, a little town in Staffordshir ... there be many smiths and bytte makers yn the towne. It longith now to the king and there is a park of that name scant half a mile from the towne. At Waulleshall be pittes of se cole, pyttes of lyme ...'

Rowley – dates back to 1173 and is not mentioned in the Domesday Book. A church was built around AD 1200 which probably signifies there was a population in the area. The church was built from 'Rowley Rag', the local stone. By 1500 Rowley Regis was named as a village in various documents.

Pelsall – has been in existence for at least 1,000 years, as Wulfrun's charter (dated AD 994) recorded land in 'Peolshale'. The Domesday Book records the land as 'waste' with half a hide owned by the Canons of Wolverhampton. In 1215–1224 a mill is mentioned at Peleshale.

The Delves – was once described as an oasis between Walsall, Wednesbury and West Bromwich. The origin of the name is unclear, but Thor, the hammer wielding Norse God of thunder, lightning, storms and oak trees (among other things), had a servant called Delve. In Viking times 'bog-iron' was dug out and smelted.

Halesowen – was made a borough in about 1232. This status remained until 1835, when the Municipal Act omitted it.

Its status was regained in 1936, but lost again when absorbed into Dudley in 1974. The Halesowen authority was less than impressed with this and issued a booklet entitled 'Last Will and Testament', recording the borough's achievements.

Withymoor – is a name associated with the large housing estate just outside Brierley Hill. The name derives from 1813, when a local scythe blade and spade maker issued his 'Withymoor' penny token.

Smethwick – is recorded in the Domesday Book, but didn't feature in history until the eighteenth century, when it was first recorded as having a church. In 1801 the population was only about 1,100. The canal and railway boom stimulated growth and the population had risen to 54,000 in 1901.

Dorothy Parkes realised Smethwick did not have its own church and so set about doing something about it, to prevent the village from collapsing into godlessness. Dorothy settled enough money and land to build a brick church with a classical tower, to be built within three years of her death. The church was completed in 1732 and Dorothy, who had been buried in Harborne churchyard, was reinterred into the church she had provided. It is said that she was the founder of modern Smethwick.

Smethwick, pronounced locally as 'Smerrick', is one of the towns whose 'Blackcountryness' may be in dispute. With West Bromwich on one side, and Birmingham on the other, where does Smethwick belong?

In 1966 the town was moved from Staffordshire to join Oldbury and Rowley Regis in the new County Borough of Warley in Worcestershire. A few years later in 1974 it became part of Sandwell; did this mean Smethwick lost its identity, its sense of significance?

Smethwick history tended to focus on Boulton and Watt, Chance's, Tangye's and perhaps a handful of other factories. But no one can deny the importance of those many residents of the rows of terraced houses who contributed to the industrial development of the region. Unfortunately, this does not answer the original question – Black Country or Birmingham?

It may be there is no answer to the question, or perhaps there are thousands of answers. So, people of Smethwick, are you Brummies or Black Country folk?

3

THE
BLACK COUNTRY

FROM RURAL BACKWATER TO
THE INDUSTRIAL REVOLUTION

Cartography began in the sixteenth century. The earliest map of the British Isles, in 1540, makes no mention of any settlement in the Black Country. Speed's 1611 map of Staffordshire shows more detail: much of the Black Country is shown in Offlow and Seisdon Hundreds; Dudley is a part of Worcestershire, except the castle; Hales Owen is a detached part of Shropshire.

There was development during the seventeenth century, but mapping was still very much in its infancy. Roads and other features started to be included and town names varied; early Sturbridge became Stourbridge and Himley had a couple of iterations from Henley to Hirnley.

By the eighteenth century, maps developed a much more recognisable style to those we see today. They were less works of art and more useful for navigation. The major change came in 1801, when the first Ordnance Survey maps were published.

It took until the twenty-first century, however, for the descriptive name 'The Black Country' to appear on the latest version of the Ordnance Survey map – and that came about only because of a local campaign to have it included.

There has been much debate about who coined the term 'Black Country' and when? This question has been explored, researched, discussed and argued, and a number of theories have been put forward. Some have contended the name relates back to the eighteenth century, because black coal was visible at the surface in places, but no use of the name itself has yet been found prior to the 1840s.

Though the debate on the 'when' continues, the 'why' does seem to be fairly obvious. The region was the largest centre for mining and industry during the period of the Industrial Revolution. No other possible interpretation comes close to matching this theory. Certainly by 1846 the name was directly associated with industry.

In 1830 William Cobbett, in his book *Rural Rides*, wrote about the 'truck' or 'tommy' system operating in the 'iron country'. The truck system (also known as 'tommy truck') was a system whereby workers were paid in whole or part with tokens, which could only be redeemed at shops owned by their employer at inflated prices. The system had existed since the fifteenth century and was outlawed in the late nineteenth century.

In 1843 Thomas Tancred, in his first report of the Midland Mining Commission on South Staffordshire, referred to the region as 'The Coalfield'. In 1838 William Hawkes Smith commented on changes in 'The South Staffordshire Mining District' since 1780.

The first recorded use of the phrase 'Black Country' that I can find came in a March 1846 report in *Lloyds London Weekly Newspaper*, reporting on the quarterly meeting of the 'Black Country Ironmasters'. The search goes on for even earlier mentions.

The year 1868 is believed to be when the phrase was first used in a book title. The book was *Walks in the Black Country and Its Green Borderland* by Elihu Burritt, the United States consul in Birmingham. By the 1860s there were many references to the use of the phrase and it appears to be widely used to describe the region.

GEOGRAPHY AND GEOLOGY LESSONS

The Black Country Boundary has never been formally defined. It is not an administrative district in its own right and originally straddled the counties of Worcestershire and Staffordshire, with the Halesowen anomaly of being in Shropshire for some time. The most 'traditional' boundary is the land under which lies the 30ft-thick Staffordshire coal seam. This was the definition used by the founders of the Black Country Society in 1967.

In 1974 the County of West Midlands was formed. This boundary totally enclosed the whole area of the 'traditional' Black Country. The four authorities of Dudley, Sandwell, Walsall and Wolverhampton all contain parts of the Black Country.

There are frequent, often heated, debates about what is in and what is out. The main areas that are 'in' are fairly obvious but the borderlands are slightly more difficult to categorise. Should Wolverhampton, Walsall and Smethwick be categorised as being 'in'? Where does Halesowen fit into the picture? Should we be examining the credentials of Stourbridge more closely?

I am not qualified to decide on a definitive answer, and suspect that the question must be one of those enigmas of English geography that will never be resolved to everyone's satisfaction. It is the only region I know where there is a well-known border of importance to its population, but many do not know for certain whether they are 'in' or not.

To answer my own question, for the purposes of this book, I take a 'Catholic' view of the border. This includes the four local authorities I have already mentioned, which means that traditional border disputes in parts of Walsall, Wolverhampton and Smethwick will not be issues for me.

One simple metaphoric border I will throw in is a personal one to everyone. If you identify yourself as having good Black Country ancestors, with roots in the region, and believe you are a Black Country 'mon' or 'womon', then you probably are.

Coal is the reason the Black Country became what it is. In Cradley the first record of coal being mined was in 1640. In the 1680s in Wednesbury, coal was dug out from beneath the topsoil. Netherton colliers could simply dig coal out of the hillside to about 100 yards without sinking a shaft. But, is all coal the same? It takes many forms and each is important in different ways. Coal was the 'black gold' of the Black Country, and it was important to be able to describe the types of coal.

Brooch (brewch) coal – was found 15ft down and was about 3ft 6ins thick. Brooch was first class house coal. It was fast-burning, produced plenty of heat and left only a tiny amount of ash.

Flying reed coal – was found below the brooch coal. It was not as good as brooch because it left more residue grey ash, but was still good house coal.

Thick coal – the most well-known coal, it was famed world-wide in coal circles. It was harder, very bright to look at and gave off excellent heat, but made dirty house coal with lots of white ash.

Heathen (haythen) coal – was difficult to sell because, while it was fast burning, it left large quantities of white ash and 'bats' in the fire grate.

The Hailstone is a Rowley Black Country legend. This monolithic structure was located on the slopes of the dolerite shelf forming part of the Rowley Hills. It is said the stone came to be because of a tremendous battle between Anglo-Saxon god Woden and Norse god Thor.

Woden, with his hounds, stood astride Rowley Hill and Thor stood on Clent Hills, surrounded by his warriors of the north. As the battle raged, Thor lifted a great boulder, placed it into his giant sling and tossed it at Woden. The boulder missed and landed within the side of the Rowley Hills.

The stone cast a shadow over all the Black Country people. Sixty feet high, it towered with a girth like the tower of an ancient castle. Locals came from all over to climb the craggy rock, knowing it was unique and precious.

Around 1879, industrialists blew up the stone. During the destruction two men, Fred Wright and Benjamin Bate, were killed. The rock was used to make roads and fireplaces around the Black Country.

Ocker Hill possibly got its name because of clay used in an early pottery business. In 1686 Dr Robert Plot, a Natural History writer described earthenware, commonly produced in Wednesbury, as being decorated with a reddish slip which they got from Tipton. The slip was ochre in colour and, until recently there were two exposures of ochre-coloured clay at Ocker Hill. Potters Lane, Wednesbury was only a mile from Ocker Hill. Not proof positive, but it does support the theory.

Willenhall was known as 'Umpshire' during the Industrial Revolution. Rumour has it that houses and pubs had holes in the wall so there was room for the hump when someone sat down. The deformities were said to have developed because of heavy labour carried out in the mines and factories before people's bodies had fully formed. There may be some truth in this.

The lock trade around Willenhall was a prevalent local business and the nature of the work was likely to cause the deformities described.

Lye Waste seems to be a funny name for a village, if you could call it that. 'The Waste' has existed since 1650, when vagabonds took possession and built mud houses. The houses were built on 'Waste Bank', a slum area overlooking the Lye itself.

The dialect in the Waste was very distinctive, even for the Black Country. It was notable for the use of Anglo-Saxon words and endings to words. For example, 'shoes' were 'shoen' and 'houses' were 'housen'. Lye residents were miners, anvil makers, bucket and bath makers and nail makers.

Gig Mill in Stourbridge derives its name from the manufacture of woollen goods. A 'gig' was a machine by which the 'shag' or 'nap' is raised on blankets and other cloth. The trade existed in 1693 and lasted for at least 200 years, until the early nineteenth century.

Hungary Hill at Stourbridge, which has a junction with the Lye to Stourbridge road, was thought to have been named after immigrant Hungarians living in the area. They were the founders of the Stourbridge glass industry; a glassworks there was mentioned in 1699.

Another suggestion was that the land may have been poor quality for agricultural purposes, making people hungry. But it was in fact valuable as a rich source of clay and coal and both were mined extensively. All we know for sure is that the name dates back a number of centuries.

Sot's 'Ole is a peculiarly named area in West Bromwich. Lloyd Street was at one point populated by working-class people. It continued on into Dagger Lane, where the housing stock consisted of more up-market residences; bungalows and stately villas. At one point, near to Hill House Farm, there is a steep dip in the terrain. This small part of Dagger Lane was known to Lloyd Street residents as Sot's 'Ole. But why?

One explanation claims it was a regular resting place for an old drunkard. Or in the early eighteenth century, there was a public house in the hollow called The Bear and Ragged Staff, that was run by Richard Reeves, aka 'Old Sot'. The area has now been built over and is known as Temple Meadows Road.

Mumpers' Dingle is another oddly named Black Country location. It has been attributed to Mumber Lane, Willenhall, but this is far from conclusive. Another theorist points to a small bridge crossing the Bentley Canal, which was known as 'Dingle Bridge' and the lane leading to it was Dingle Lane. The final piece of 'evidence' for this theory is that the field opposite was called 'Dingle Piece'.

Picturedrome Way, Darlaston, marks the site of Darlaston's first cinema, 'The Picturedrome'. It opened in May 1911 and closed its doors for the last time in 1959. I cannot find any other road name in the Black Country named after a cinema.

Whynot Street, Cradley is named on the 1881 Ordnance Survey, and in a trade directory in 1873 there is mention of beer retailer G. Partridge of the Why Not Call and See. The public house has since been renamed the Why Not Inn, and it is from this that the street name derives.

Did J.R.R. Tolkien take inspiration from the Black Country? The great author was born at the turn of the twentieth century and went on to write about Middle Earth, his own fantasy world. Through his first book *The Hobbit*, the three volumes of the *Lord of the Rings* trilogy, and other works such as *The Silmarillion*, Tolkien painted word pictures of epic proportions, but from where did he draw his ideas?

It is well known that the Cole Valley and Sarehole Mill in Birmingham formed part of his inspiration, but what about the Black Country? Were the mines of Moria based on the many examples of mines that pockmarked the industrial landscape?

The fantasy images of Orthanc, where Wizard Saruman makes his evil denizens work in mines and foundries, evokes images for me of the Black Country at the height of the Industrial Revolution; described as 'Black by Day and Red by Night'.

Tolkien describes Mordor as the 'black land'. Elihu Burritt used the phrase to describe the Black Country. Tolkien also described the language of Mordor as 'black speech'; one of many languages created in his works.

Did he use the Black Country dialect as his inspiration for 'black speech', or any other Middle Earth language? Did he bear in mind the fact that the Black Country dialect is one of the last examples of early English still being spoken?

How Come Dudley Has a Port?

Here is a message for all shipping in the Dudley area – there is no sea! Yet, Dudley has its own port. It was a canal port and dates back to the eighteenth century. Canals were becoming an easy and profitable way of transporting goods, and Dudley, situated on high ground, didn't lend itself to canal improvement.

Locks from the town to canals on the lower levels were seen as impracticable, so, in Coneygre, as business advanced there began to develop something like a port. Wharves and warehouses lined the canal and the area soon assumed the name 'Dudley's Port'.

WHO SAID WHAT?

One observer of the nail making trade in 1741 was a man called Hutton:

I was surprised by the number of blacksmiths shops ... In some of those shops I observed one or more females, stripped of their upper garment and not overcharged with their lower, wielding the hammer with all the grace of the sex. The beauties of their faces were rather eclipsed by the smut of the anvil.

Even 100 years later, Dudley was deemed to be the centre of the trade, and women were still using the same techniques. Thomas Carlyle wrote in 1824:

A frightful scene ... a dense cloud of pestilential smoke hangs over it forever ... and at night the whole region burns like a volcano spitting fire from a thousand tubes of brick.

But oh the wretched thousands of mortals who grind out their destiny there!

In 1841 Charles Dickens wrote in *The Old Curiosity Shop* of our homeland. He called it a black region, 'where not a blade of grass was seen to grow, where not a bud put forth its promise in the spring, where nothing green could live but on the surface of a stagnant pool'.

Dickens also eloquently described The Swan in the market place in Wolverhampton and wrote of his visit to the town in 1853: 'The Swan is confident about its soup, is troubled with no distrust concerning cod fish, speaks the word of promise in relation to an enormous chine of roast beef...' He was describing an Ironmasters dinner, to which he had been invited.

The sound of the Black Country has changed in the last forty years, what do we miss:

Pump, pump, pump! Goes the engine all night, to get out the water that soaks in all day. Clatter, clatter, bink a tink, whistle and screech go the chains and the whimsy bell all day long. Up and down bobs the skip from morning till night, laden with the spoils of the mine ... Up and down, down and up, moves the iron arm, and it never tires ...

(Reverend J.B. Owen MA, 1856)

In the 1860s the American Elihu Burritt wrote of the region. From Dudley Castle he saw 'The sublimest battle scene on earth' and contrasted fire, smoke, cloud and the moon in his writing.

Much of Francis Brett Young's writing drew upon personal experience. His choice of region is made clear in a speech he gave in Brierley Hill in 1940:

The England for which I feel most tenderly is that part of the country in which I was born: The Black Country. It may not be particularly beautiful. We do not claim that for it. But we can say that the Black Country is the very heart of England and that the people who inhabit it and speak its language are the soundest, kindliest, and toughest to be found in this island.

In 1933 J.B. Priestley wrote about his visit to the Black Country:

The places I saw had names, but these names were merely so much alliteration: Wolverhampton, Wednesbury, Wednesfield and Walsall. You could call them all wilderness, and have done with it. I never knew where one ended and another began.

Back as long ago as 1952, Phil Drabble wrote that the Black Country was becoming no more than a memory. He said that for one thing it was no longer black. There is plenty of evidence of the 'green country' all around the region, but many elements of our former industrial heritage are still in existence.

4

THE FIRST AND THE LAST …

FIRSTS

The first Methodist Chapel built in South Staffordshire was built in Tipton in 1755.

The *Aaron Manby* was the world's first iron steamboat, built in 1822 at Tipton and named after one of the maker's partners. The boat was fitted with revolving oars, invented by John Oldham. The iron plate used was ¼in thick with ribs of standard angle iron and the *Manby*'s funnel was 47ft high. The boat was 106ft long and 17ft broad.

Once built, the *Manby* was dismantled and transported by canal to London, where it was re-assembled at Rotherhithe. *The Morning Chronicle* of 14 May 1822 said: 'She is the most complete piece of workmanship in the iron way that has ever been witnessed.'

The *Manby* sailed to Boulogne, taking 55 hours. It then went on to Le Havre and Rouen. It carried Pig iron and iron castings and the boat took on a consignment of clover seed at Rouen. The *Manby* remained in France and was still at work in 1842. It is believed it was broken up in 1855.

The first locomotive to run on rails in America was made in Stourbridge. Horatio Allen came to England in January 1828 to make enquiries about the use and power of railway engines. He visited the Newcastle works of the Stephenson family, who were unable to supply the four locomotives that Allen wanted.

Allen went to Stourbridge, and the ironworks of John Bradley & Co., where John Urpeth Rastrick and James Foster were more able to assist. They were working on an engine, the Agenoria, now the star exhibit in the Railway Museum at York. Allen negotiated a deal for three engines.

Stephenson did manage to deliver the first engine to New York, but Allen waited for the first Black Country engine. The Stourbridge Lion was the first to run on rails on 3 miles of track at Honesdale, crossing the Lackawaxen Creek on a trestle bridge some 30ft above the creek.

The Lion's relics are owned by the Smithsonian Institute in Washington and the boiler and some parts are on display in the Baltimore & Ohio Railway Museum.

The first police station in Dudley was in Priory Street, opposite the Saracen's Head. It has probably been there since 1847. The current station was built in 1940 and there were plans to demolish the old building. This never happened and the imposing old station is still there, with its crenelated towers. It now forms part of the main council buildings, and still has those magnificent features.

The first fire 'engine' in Darlaston in 1896 was a hand pump drawn by two horses. Their names were 'Nobby' and 'Hell-Fire Jack'. I wonder if Jack was the 'God of Hell-Fire' from the song by Arthur Brown (1968) and his band 'The Crazy World of Arthur Brown'.

On 13 April 1907, the first kick in the inaugural Schoolboy International football match was made by the Mayor of Walsall, Alderman B. Dean. The match was played in Walsall at the Hillary Street ground; Walsall was the venue because of the enthusiasm of Walsall Education Committee, the Secretary of Walsall Schools' FA and the aforementioned mayor.

The weather for the match was not good, with heavy rainfall during the morning, but an undaunted crowd of 2,500 attended. The result was 3–1 to England, and as England departed the field the band played 'See the Conquering Hero Comes'.

The idea of international school football was first discussed in 1906.

Another footballing first involved Joseph Heath, who was responsible for his sporting achievement on Saturday 14 September 1891. The venue was the Molineux, Wolverhampton, where Wolverhampton Wanderers were playing Accrington Stanley. An Accrington player handled the ball to prevent a goal being scored. Up stepped Heath and scored the second goal in what would be a 5–0 thrashing of the visitors. Nothing unusual, except that this was the first goal scored from a penalty kick on any English football ground.

The penalty law had been in place in the Irish and Scottish leagues, but it had only been adopted by the English FA in September 1891.

The first recorded Black Country Blast Furnace crown is in some doubt. The first were said to have been in (West) Bromwich, Cradley, Hales (Owen), Himley and Rushall in the late sixteenth century. These were all charcoal furnaces and timber began to rapidly disappear across the region with their arrival.

Abraham Darby is attributed as the man who first produced pig iron in a blast furnace using coke, in 1709. He was born at Old Farm Lodge, off Wren's Nest Hill in 1678. However, Dud Dudley also has a stake in Darby's claim. You will read about Dud later ...

Wolverhampton's first motorist was Thomas Parker. He is one of those innovators who are largely forgotten, despite changing people's lives in a number of ways. Not only did he develop an early electrical distribution system for lighting streets and homes, but he also invented smokeless fuel and was responsible for electrically powered trams and trains.

Parker built his first car in 1884 and within a few years he was driving daily from his home in Tettenhall to Wolverhampton.

Parker's first real invention was in 1876, a steam pump, which eventually sold worldwide. A couple of years later he designed and built a dynamo, one of the first in the country to be used in industry. His list of inventions include: the 'Kyrle' open grate; improvements on a lead-acid cell for batteries; alternators and equipment for the electric tramway in Portrush, Northern Ireland.

Parker also constructed an electrical plant for Blackpool Tramway, and claimed to have developed an electrically powered vehicle as early as 1884. More motor vehicle innovation included four-wheel steering and all round hydraulic brakes.

In Lye the first motorised vehicle was seen on the roads in 1898. Its owner was a colourful character, Dr H. Christopher Darby, and his mode of transport is reputed to have been a DeDion-Bouton tri-cycle. Doctor Darby had a practice on Stourbridge Road, where he had competition from another medical man, Doctor Edwin Webster Hardwicke of Lye Cross.

Darby and Harwicke each called the other 'The opposition', never using the other's name. It is said, however, that their wives were on good terms with each other. Hardwicke had a world-famous son, the actor Sir Cedric Hardwicke.

The first powered flight to be made in the Black Country was Spencer's Great Airship, billed as the latest development of aerial navigation.

The airship was 80ft long, 35ft in diameter and held 40,000 square foot of gas. It made its appearance at the 13th Grand Annual Fetes and Flower Show at Corbett Hospital in August 1905.

Stanley Spencer was the 'pilot' who, by the time of the fetes, had already made thirty-eight previous airship flights, seven in this balloon. When the maiden Black Country flight was made, there was not a breath of wind. The ship rose like a bird, made its ascent and sailed off towards Brierley Hill. An approaching storm caused Spencer to make his descent at the golf links at Scotts Green.

The following day another successful ascent was made, again drifting on a light breeze towards Brierley Hill.

The first woman brewery owner was Black Country brewess Julia Hanson, also the first woman to give her name to a brewery company. In 1871 Julia ran her business at Tower Street, Dudley, following the death of her husband Thomas.

Julia traded as 'Mrs Julia Hanson, Wine and Spirit Merchant'. When she died in 1894 her sons took on the business, purchasing the Peacock Hotel and brewery in Upper High Street, as well as several public houses. In 1902 the company was registered as Julia Hanson and Sons Limited.

It is reputed that Tipton was the first town in England to have street lights installed.

The world's first stainless steel toast rack was made in 1928 at the Old Hall Works in Bloxwich. Two years later William Wiggin made the world's first stainless steel teapot, again at the Old Hall Works. Now if they could only make a teapot that poured without spilling or dripping!

The first recorded wireless transmission in the Black Country took place on 19 April 1910. Howard Littley of West Bromwich made the transmission from his home in Lodge Road, West Bromwich. Littley was aged 18 and made the transmission to the family iron foundry at Swan Village.

The Morse code transmissions were received by Mr H. Clark, who had been trained by Howard to receive them. A reply was sent by Clark: 'I have received your message loud and clear, heartiest congratulations on the result of your experiments.'

Howard's station had a steam-driven generator, a 76ft-high mast and a 520 volt lead-acid battery. In the 1930s Littley moved to 'Radiohm', Bridgnorth Road, Stourton. Mains electricity was available for power, but the old 520 volt battery was kept in Howard's bathroom for emergency supplies.

The first telephones in the Black Country were installed in Wolverhampton. One was in July 1880 and enabled the Reliance Hemp and Flax Mills, Brick Kiln Street in Wolverhampton to be connected to a civil engineers office, named Watkins, in High Street. Another was said to connect Graisley Old Hall in Claremont Road with Ironmongers' Rope Factory in Salop Street.

By October 1880 the first Wolverhampton telephone exchange had been set up in Garrick Street.

Graisley Old Hall may well be the oldest residential building in Wolverhampton, with parts of the building pre-dating 1485. Or the honour could go to Merridale Old Farm, which has features that could date back to the twelfth century.

The world's first axle was made at the Patent Shaft Works in Wednesbury. Its originator was Reverend James Hardy, who invented the faggoted axle of forged iron, patented in 1835.

Wednesbury-born Sir William Maddock Bayliss discovered the first hormone in 1902. Bayliss was educated in Wolverhampton and at the University College London. He was apprenticed to a doctor in Wolverhampton, but didn't complete his training.

Bayliss, along with his brother-in-law Ernest Starling, discovered secretin. He made his discovery after taking a teaching post at UCL but it was not without controversy; the team used animals in their experiments and Bayliss was accused of having vivisected a brown dog. This led to a libel case, which Bayliss won, donating the damages to the college for research. A memorial was erected to the brown dog in Battersea, which some medical students attacked, leading to the worst riots in London until the Poll Tax riots in the 1980s.

Stourbridge was one of the first country towns to have a private bank. William Blow Collis opened what came to be known as the 'Old Bank'. An early client was James Foster (of Agenoria and Stourbridge Lion fame). Foster was in dispute with the bank over the re-paying of a £5,000 debt, so he went to his iron works, loaded £5,000 in cash into a wheelbarrow, took it to the bank and tipped it onto the floor – debt repaid!

Three years later, Foster had the last laugh when he became the banks owner, which evolved into the Midland Bank and now HSBC. This was first formed as the Birmingham and Midland Bank, which absorbed the Old Bank as part of its expansion.

Lloyds Bank opened their first branch at Oldbury in 1864. The Lloyds business originated in Dale End, Birmingham, and the first branch opened because they wanted to service one of their best industrial customers with their wage money. The branch, in Birmingham Street, is still there today.

On the subject of money, Coseley-born Harry Eccleston, OBE, was the first artist designer for the Bank of England, a post he held from 1958 to 1983. He designed the series 'D' notes, which came into circulation in 1970. Some of his iconic portraits that appeared on the bank notes in your purse or wallet were a portrait of Her Majesty the Queen, the Duke of Wellington, Florence Nightingale, William Shakespeare and Christopher Wren.

Eccleston retained his strong Black Country roots and the area provided inspiration throughout his life. He painted the landscape, industry and the people; one of his works reflected the popular activity of pigeon racing.

Wolverhampton was the first town centre in Britain to be fitted with CCTV cameras in 1988.

LAST

The last Black Country bellow maker was Syd Royall from Tividale, who spent fifty-five years working the trade, from 1935 to 1990. He was 14 when he started as an apprentice.

Syd worked at Vaughan's (Hope Works) Ltd. The company was a family concern, until it was acquired by Folkes Group in the early 1970s. The business was making and renovating bellows of all sizes.

There was a decline in the need for foundry bellows in the 1940s and at one stage Syd was told he might soon be made redundant. However, there was enough work to keep him going until 1990, though he became a one man band.

As time went on, Syd became a master in his craft, restoring handsome, ornate, carved fireside bellows. He was much sought after, as his skill was dying out.

The last mud house in Lye Waste was only knocked down in 1962.

The last example of Deep Coal Mining in the Black Country came in March 1968, with the closure of Baggeridge Colliery. The first shaft had been sunk in 1899, but it took a lot money to make the mine workable due to the depth of the seam (600 yards) and the difficulties of flooding. It was described as a 'mighty financial undertaking' for its owner, the Earl of Dudley.

In 1965 Hampstead Colliery in Great Barr had been the penultimate deep coal mine to close.

The last nailer in Gornal was James March. His shop was in Hopyard Lane and he retired in 1922.

The last ever woman chain maker (by hand) was Lucy Woodall. She retired 22 December 1972. She began work in 1913 as an apprentice chain maker, working 67 hours a week. By the age of 15 she was working on piecework rates. In her youth her only breaks were to go hop picking. Lucy died in 1979, aged 80.

When Lucy started work she suffered the same initiation as other workers. She was sent for a 9in ruler, a left-handed spanner and the handle of her bellows was coated in mud – nothing changes.

The last ever horse race at Walsall Race Course was won by a horse called 'Bloxwich', which was trained at Hednesford. The racecourse was situated between Walsall Brook and the mill stream, at Long Meadow. It opened in 1777 and a grandstand was opened in 1809.

Netherton Tunnel was the last canal tunnel to be built during the Canal Age. It opened in 1858 and is 3,027 yards (2,768m) long. Today it is billed as the longest car-free tunnel you can go through on a bike! It is wider than most tunnels, so that towpaths could be built on both sides to speed up the passage of barges.

5

THE SIZE DEBATE

LARGEST

The fattest man in the Black Country was undoubtedly George Lovatt. Famous 'large' people in history include Peter Yarnall of East Ham, (59 stone, 374kg) and Leicester's Daniel Lambert (52 stone, 330kg). The Black Country heavyweight contender came from Round Oak, Brierley Hill and died in 1933, aged 63.

It is said that Lovatt weighed 42 stone (267kg) at the time he died. He was notable not only for his weight, he also founded the Chainmakers' and Strikers' Association in 1889.

George Lovatt's coffin makers were their family friends, the Wheeler's. In the past they had made a very large stool and an extra-strong bed for him from ash. At George's funeral thousands of people turned out to see the spectacle.

Simply getting the coffin from the house required the removal of railings and a bay window. A block and tackle was required to lift George. His coffin was over 7ft long, 27ins deep and 42½ins wide. The cortege was headed by two mounted policemen. It took twenty men some 20 minutes to remove the coffin from its wagon and place it onto a bier to wheel it into St Michael's Church, Brierley Hill, where George is buried.

The West Bromwich Giant was Walter Parsons, who was born about 1580 into a family of blacksmiths. West Bromwich at the time was a mere small hamlet and Parsons' family came from the Hall End district. Parsons became a blacksmith's assistant, but he grew so tall that his employer was 'forced to digg a hole in the ground for him to stand in up to his knees, when he struck at the anvil, or sawed wood with another, that he might be at a level with his fellow-workman'.

Documents tell us that Parsons' height ranged from 7ft 6ins to 9ft, though the latter is probably an extreme exaggeration. At this time the Royal Court had a habit of hiring various servants who had unusual features, such as dwarves or giants.

When news of the giant Parsons reached the royal ears of King James I of England (James VI of Scotland), he had him brought to London where Parsons became the King's porter. He is said to have had strength equal to his height, valour to his strength and temper to his valour. In other words, like many giants, he was gentle in nature.

Once, however, when walking through London, a man of normal height 'affronted' Parsons. He responded by lifting him up by the waistband of his breeches and hung him onto one of the hooks of the shambles to be ridiculed by the people.

It is said that Parsons remained in office and served Charles I, until Parson's death in the late 1620s. The facts of Parsons stature and height are well-documented in historical texts, and there were a number of portraits painted of him in London.

The largest Woolworth store in Europe used to be the one in the Mander Centre, Wolverhampton, or at least it was in 1965.

The largest and oldest established church with a mainly African-Caribbean congregation in the Black Country was The New Testament Church of God, which was founded in 1952 in Wolverhampton.

Wombourne, on the fringe of the Black Country, claims to be the largest village in England. In 2001 it had a population of 13,691 and has existed since Anglo-Saxon times.

In 1892 the largest sausage maker in the world was Palethorpe's of Dudley Port. The company was founded in 1850 and moved away from the Black Country in 1967.

The largest anchor in the world, for decades after it was built, was the anchor for the *Titanic* made in 1911. It was labelled as such by Blocksidge's 'Dudley Almanack' in 1912, and had been made by Noah Hingley of Netherton. The anchor weighed 16 tons and twelve men took three weeks to make it. Its total length was 15ft; not bad for a region that is as far away from the coast as anywhere in the UK.

In 2010 a replica anchor was made as part of a TV documentary, it also weighed in at 16 tons. For a time the replica was on display at the Black Country Living Museum. Its permanent home is now in the centre of Netherton, opposite Netherton Arts Centre.

Many other items used on the RMS *Titanic* were made in the Black Country. These included smaller bower anchors and chain. Lifeboat davits were made at Harts Hill. Glass tableware, jugs, decanters, salt cellars and wine glasses were all made at Stourbridge by Stuart Crystal.

The *Titanic* anchor's record as the largest in the world has since been broken. The heaviest anchor I could find details for weighed 36 tons, for a super tanker built in 1979, the *Seawise Giant*, which is generally considered the largest ship ever built.

The largest electric power installation in England was said to be Ocker Hill Power Station in Tipton. At the time of its construction in 1902, it was planned that it would be the largest in England. It had three cooling towers, which were demolished in 1985, and the power station finally closed in 1977. Housing has since been built on the site.

The biggest spud award goes to ... who knows? The record size for a humble potato was 18lb 4oz, set by a man from Chester in 1795. In October 1905 a new record was claimed in the *Dudley Herald*, a potato weighing 28lb 8oz. The claim may not have much credibility beyond the newspaper report.

Walsall had the largest solo mural painting in the world, according to *BBC Midlands Today* in 2007. It was 'Hole in the wall' in Upper Rushall Street, and depicted Walsall scenes. It was painted by local graffiti artist CHU, took forty-two working days to complete and covered 2,800 square feet.

SMALLEST

The smallest Urban District Council in the Black Country was Amblecote UDC. It had the smallest population of any UDC in the country, with only 3,000 residents. It had no coat of arms, but acquired a badge of office, which depicted its main trades of glassmaking, engineering and brick making. It disappeared in the 1966 local government changes.

Speed isn't everything mind. One of the smallest cars ever built came from Wolverhampton. It was the 'Atomette', manufactured by Allan Thomas in Cleveland Street. Maybe the name conjures up images of speed and power, but this was not the case. The engine was a 2½hp two-stroke model, made by Villiers with a three-speed gearbox. It was big enough to carry two people.

The car was built in 1922 and a road test concluded 'a short run on the machine in single-seat form revealed its ample leg room and an ability to travel at 25–30mph'. (I think this was before Jeremy Clarkson began his career as a motoring journalist!)

The complete car weighed in at 2½cwt (127kg) and a selling point was that it could easily be lifted up a step if needed. The cost was 90 Guineas (£94.50) and fuel economy was 90 miles per gallon. Nothing is recorded about sales of the vehicle.

LONGEST

The longest family connection to a pub in the Black Country must surely go to the Cox family, who held the licence for The Round of Beef at Colley Gate for 138 years, from Edwin Cox in 1844 to Norman Cox in 1982. One of the Cox's, Harry, played cricket for Colley Gate and had a reputation as an attacking batsman, often accompanying his shot with a loud cry of 'osher'.

Norman Cox was the last of his family to hold the licence, from 1953 to 1976. Before him, his father had held the licence for fifty-two years and his grandfather for forty-seven. Norman was the end of the Cox line for the job of licensee.

Keith Boxley of Wombourne made the longest continuous sausage in 1988. It was 21.12km in length and he is still looking for a baker who can make a roll to put it in!

HIGHEST

The highest parish church in the country is said to be St Andrew's in Netherton, at 650ft above sea level. It was built in 1830. My research shows it is probably not in the top ten in the country. St Thomas's, 'Top' Church in Dudley is 690ft, Rowley Regis Church is 700ft, and Sedgley Church (near to Sedgley Beacon at 778ft) are all higher than St Andrew's.

Galton Bridge at Smethwick was built in the late 1820s by Thomas Telford. It was the highest canal bridge in the world at the time it was built and has a span of 151ft (46m). It is now a pedestrian bridge and is also a Grade 1 listed building.

If you look east from the top of Sedgley Beacon, your next highest point will be the Ural Mountains in Western Russia, something that can be said of many of the highest points in the region. Its height above sea level is 781ft (238m). Barr Beacon is not far behind, measuring 745ft (227m). On a clear day you can see eleven counties, including Powys in Wales.

OLDEST

The Leathern Bottle in Wednesbury is said to be the oldest pub in the Black Country.

The Manor House, just outside West Bromwich, is one of the oldest buildings in the Black Country that is still in use. Known locally as 'Old Hall', it is one of the most complete examples of a medieval timber-framed building.

The local corporation wanted to demolish the building in the 1960s, but were persuaded they had a national treasure and restored it. The house is currently opened for events on special occasions.

The oldest document in Walsall is an undated parchment, written in Latin and likely to have been written in about AD 1240. It is a charter, a grant of rights, by William Ruffus, Lord of the Manor of Walsall. The document is addressed to the burgesses of the town, exempting them from all feudal services and taxes, except 'tallage', a feudal tax on towns and boroughs.

Its importance lies in the fact that it is the first such grant of rights and privileges, and the first evidence of the existence of the Borough of Walsall. A burgess was a citizen of a borough with full rights; in other words a leading citizen and property holder.

The oldest Operatic Society in the Black Country is CHAOS (Cradley Heath, Old Hill and District Amateur Operatic Society), formed in 1908. It was set up to raise money for charities and 'educating the public'.

English light opera was popular because of the likes of Gilbert and Sullivan. The first opera produced by the Society was *HMS Pinafore* at the Empire Theatre, Cradley Heath. This had opened in 1905. Their next performance was in 1910, again a Gilbert and Sullivan, this time *The Gondoliers*.

The Society is still active today. The only time they had no productions was during the periods covered by the First and Second World Wars. The Empire had, in 1910, been the venue for meetings during the women chainmakers' strike. It closed its doors in 1937.

EVERYTHING ELSE

Could it be that the deepest well in Britain is located at Smestow Bridge? It is 2,842ft deep and was built in 1912 by Germans.

Reg Morris from Walsall has set a number of world records, according to the Guinness Book of Records, between 1985 and 1988. These were the records for brick carrying, fastest sausage meat eating, most flame torches extinguished in the mouth and fastest kipper eating – not all at the same time mind!

In 2004 MENSA's youngest member was 6-year-old Chloe Bennion of Wednesfield. Her IQ was 138. Since then though, in 2006, 2-year-old Georgina Brown beat her record, and in 2009 Elise Tan Roberts, also aged 2, was admitted to the ranks of the uber-brainy.

The heaviest load ever carried by British Rail was a 122ft long boiler drum, which weighed 240 tons. The drum was made in Ettingshall and transported to Yorkshire in 1965.

6

STATUES AND MONUMENTS

The statue of Prince Albert that stands in Queen's Square, Wolverhampton, was sculpted by Thomas Thorneycroft. Another major piece of his work is a statue of the first mayor of the town, G.B. Thorneycroft. The two are apparently not related. When Queen Victoria unveiled Albert's statue in 1866, it was her first public appearance for five years following the death of her beloved Prince Albert.

The first statue of Sister Dora was erected in 1886, eight years after her death. Dr MacLachlan, the first medical officer for Walsall, had taken plaster casts of her face and 'powerful maternal hands' the day after she died. One thousand, two hundred pounds was raised towards the statue, many donations from local workers through collections. Francis Williamson carved the statue from white Sicilian marble and it was unveiled by the Mayor of Walsall in October 1886.

By the middle of the last century, pollution had badly eroded the marble and a second fund was started to cast a replica in bronze. This was unveiled in 1957, the 125th anniversary of Dora's birth. This is the statue which stands proudly in The Bridge at Walsall.

In 1888 the statue of the first Earl of Dudley was erected at the top of Castle Hill, and stands proud in the lea of Dudley Castle. Until 1939 the Earl faced the Conservative Club below St Edmunds Church.

A road improvement scheme necessitated a move for the statue of 6 yards, to allow a new dual carriageway to be built.

When the statue was replaced in the centre of the traffic island, he was turned to face the Market Place. This was at the request of the then present earl, and also to 'even out wear on the statue'.

A statue of William Perry, the 'Tipton Slasher' stands just a few yards from the Fountain Inn in Tipton. Perry used the Fountain as his headquarters and so the site of the statue in Coronation Gardens seemed appropriate. The remains of William Perry were allegedly removed from St John's Church at Kates Hill in the 1970s, and placed in the footings of the statue.

The statue was designed by local artist Bill Haynes, cost £25,000 and was unveiled in 1993. The grave of the 'Slasher' shows no signs of having been tampered with, so it seems unlikely that the remains were removed.

Duncan Edwards' Statue stands proud in Dudley Market Place. Duncan is one of Dudley's most famous sporting heroes. He was born in 1936 and played football for Manchester United. He was one of the Busby Babes who died in the Munich air disaster in February 1958 and his statue was unveiled by his mother and Sir Bobby Charlton in 1999.

A bronze horse, based on the mythological winged horse Pegasus, sits grandly on Scott's Green island, opposite Holly Hall School, just outside Dudley. It stands 7m high and was made by Andrew Logan, commissioned for the new millennium. Pegasus signifies hope for the future. Glass inlay on the wings refers to the Stourbridge glass industry and the plinth was made locally. It was unveiled in 2001 by the Mayor of Dudley, John Walters; Zandra Rhodes and the sculptor were also present.

A controversial statue of Princess Diana, given to Walsall, struggled to find a home in 2000. The black granite statue was destined for the new bus station in the town. It was the Home Secretary, Jack Straw, who wrote to Walsall council in October 2000, saying it was not possible to make a favourable recommendation to Her Majesty for the statue.

The future of the £16,000 statue, carved by craftsmen in India and paid for by a monumental mason in Walsall, was in doubt. Some local councillors supported the statue, but the leader, Mike Bird, called it 'demonic'. The statue now stands outside the premises of the creator, at his funeral parlour in Bloxwich; it has been re-painted.

7

ROYAL
VISITS

In 1575, Queen Elizabeth I was an early royal visitor to Dudley. She was received by Edward Dudley at Dudley Castle. Her visit was a grand affair and our 'Virgin Queen' was wined and dined in the castle. She moved on to Hartlebury and then to Worcester.

Ten years later the castle was considered for its suitability as a prison for Mary Queen of Scots, prior to her trial for treason, but its facilities did not come up to the required standard. Instead she was sent to Fotheringay Castle.

In 1645 King Charles I was in the region during the English Civil War. On 15 May he stayed at Himley Hall and on the 16th he was stationed at Bushbury, near to Prince Rupert's Wolverhampton Headquarters. In January 1649, Charles was tried and executed by being beheaded.

Not exactly a planned royal visit was that of Charles II's flight after the Battle of Worcester in 1651, during the English Civil War. During his escape he went to Boscobel House, where he famously hid in an oak tree. He ended his trip in Bentley, his host being Colonel Lane. Bentley was in Staffordshire and was enemy territory; the county was under Parliamentary control.

Charles's escape was with the assistance of Jane Lane, sister of the Colonel. He was disguised as her servant for their journey to Bristol

In 1810 it is believed that King George IV visited Bilston incognito. He is said to have toured Wilkinson's Works and gone down a local pit.

In 1866 Queen Victoria visited Wolverhampton to unveil the statue of her beloved Albert. A triumphal arch of coal was built at the railway station to welcome Her Majesty.

On 22 May 1894 Queen Victoria passed through the Black Country on the Royal Train en route to Manchester, to open the new ship canal. Folklore has it that the Queen drew the blinds of her compartment while travelling through the Black Country.

In July 1900 the Duke and Duchess of York were guests of the Mander family at Wightwick Manor. The couple would become King George V and Queen Mary. George came to the throne in 1910, following the death of Edward VII, and reigned for almost twenty-six years.

On 16 June 1923 the Prince of Wales, later King Edward VIII, visited the Black Country. He was presented with a miniature chain and anchor by Benjamin Hodgetts of Cradley, who worked for Noah Hingley's of Netherton.

In 1925 the Duke and Duchess of York visited Royal Brierley Crystal, the first of three royal visits to the works over the years. Another visit to Royal Brierley Crystal was by Princess Margaret in 1960. (The third is documented on the following page.)

In 1927 the Duke of Kent visited Dudley to officially open the new council offices. The visit was hosted by the youngest ever Mayor of Dudley, Kates Hill businessman Joseph Hillman.

Prince George, the next Duke of Kent, visited Dudley in February 1941. He went to the Market Place where he met personnel from the Home Guard and ARP Wardens. The Duke sadly died in an air crash in August 1942 in northern Scotland, whilst he was en route to Iceland.

On 1 May 1951 Princess Margaret visited Walsall to lay the first stone of the Church Hill war memorial garden.

Queen Elizabeth and Prince Philip visited Dudley on 23 April 1957. The royal couple had lunch at the Town Hall. Later in the afternoon they moved on to Brierley Hill.

On 24 May 1962 the Queen paid a visit to Walsall. She visited Crabtree's Lincoln Works in Beacon Street. This was the first visit to the town by a reigning monarch. Her Majesty toured the Crabtree Works and was presented with a pair of silver bowls. It was a memorable day for the thousands of visitors who attended the visit.

In 1983 Princess Anne performed the opening ceremony of the Baggeridge Country Park, on the site of the former Baggeridge Colliery, the last important pit in the Black Country.

On 23 July 1985 Diana, Princess of Wales visited Royal Brierley Crystal. She arrived by helicopter, landing at Stephens Park; I was a proud police constable on duty at the landing. Diana was presented with a posy and a solid glass Noah's Ark as a memento of her visit.

On 24 October 1986 the Duke of Gloucester visited the Black Country Living Museum to open the new entrance building.

In 1991 Princess Diana visited the Relate offices in Lower Hall Lane, Walsall. She was the patron of the charity. Diana was late because she had diverted en route to visit friends to comfort them over their child. She also visited the new £24 million Walsall Manor Hospital.

Queen Elizabeth II visited Tipton on 24 June 1994; this was the first visit to the town by a reigning monarch. She opened the new Jobcentre in Owen Street.

The death of Queen Victoria in 1901 was marked by the cancellation of events around the Black Country. Wolverhampton steeplechases, theatre programmes at Walsall, a banquet at Wordsley and the Batchelor's Ball at Stourbridge Town Hall were all either cancelled or postponed.

An early Royal impersonator (does this count?) became such by accident. Matilda Devall lived at Kates Hill, Dudley. By all accounts she was a formidable character, but also had a good sense of humour.

In 1897 Matilda attended a funeral in Dudley and afterwards made her way back home. This particular evening a huge bonfire was being held to celebrate the 60th anniversary of Queen Victoria's accession to the throne. Matilda went to see the spectacle dressed in her funeral clothes.

People began to stare, and one or two women curtsied. It took a while for the penny to drop. Matilda looked remarkably like the pictures of Queen Victoria that people had seen and she amused the crowd by 'acting the part' of the sovereign. Matilda was asked for a repeat performance on a number of future occasions, but she steadfastly declined.

8

CRIME AND PUNISHMENT

Before the police came along, towns had to make their own arrangements to fight crime and keep order. For example, in 1814 the Bloxwich Association for the Prosecution of Felons came into being. The society offered rewards to anyone who caught a thief and returned the property.

A locally appointed constable was often the only person available to carry out a service that we take for granted today

Before 1829, and the beginnings of the police, advertisements regarding the recovery of property were common. One of our most infamous criminals, Jonathan Wild, made a living out of recovering stolen property and you can read about his exploits later in this chapter.

The first professional police force in the Black Country was formed in Walsall. Many people know that the first force in the country was the Metropolitan (not counting organisations such as the Bow Street Runners). The Met was founded in 1829 by Sir Robert Peel.

Walsall police officers first paraded for duty on 6 July 1832. Its strength consisted of a superintendent

(FH West) and three other officers. Two years later, Walsall was also the first Black Country town to have a police force under the 1834 Municipal Corporation Act; it was formed in 1835, four years before any other Black Country town.

Sergeant Childs was a member of the Walsall Police. He was on duty in 1857, during the period of a strike by miners in Bilston. He described an incident when 1,000 of the strikers descended on Walsall, intent on looting. The police formed a cordon across their path and drew their cutlasses. The miners did an 'about turn' and never returned.

A Dudley Constabulary force formed in 1840, when 'respectable townsmen formed a section of our guardian angels'. This was a result of the fear of Chartist activity. To summon the twenty or so townsmen the bells of St Thomas's Church were to be rung.

The Chartists did not appear around Dudley to incite 'The idle, ignorant and dissolute' and sometime later this group of what we would probably today term as Special Constables was disbanded. The town didn't have a proper force until 1845, when it became part of Worcestershire Constabulary.

In 1857 a Dudley Police Constable, Alfred Evens (PC 119), was charged by Supt Jewkes with neglect of duty. Evans was on duty at Wolverhampton Street in Dudley and was supposed to meet his Sergeant every half an hour; the first three meetings took place but none after that. Sgt Roberts found him in a nearby beer shop drunk and incapable.

In 1845 the House of Commons described an incident as: 'a disgrace to the magistrates and the laws of the country'. What was it that caused such uproar? On 3 April six months pregnant Eliza Price was involved in a 'push and shove' incident at Kingswinford Magistrates with Joseph Newey. Price was removed from the room by a policeman. She applied for a summons against Newey for assault, for which he was fined and bound over. However, Newey also obtained a warrant against Price for abusive behaviour.

Price was arrested by Constables Onions and Baker who marched her to Brierley Hill, despite appeals from her husband and a parish constable to release her to appear at court the following morning. Baker chained Price in front of the fire at the Horseshoes Inn (on the site of the Moor Centre), with only a wooden bench. Price was later discharged from court for the offence.

In a subsequent enquiry the magistrate was exonerated of ill-will, but criticised for not rebuking the constables. Baker was found to have 'acted from a mistaken sense of duty'. There is no mention anywhere of compensation or an apology to Mrs Price.

Police humour is well known and practical jokes common. In Dudley Borough Police Station one night, six officers were playing cards in the charge room during their refreshment break. A constable delivering a stray pony (stray horses are still a common occurrence even in twenty-first century Dudley) decided to introduce a new player to the card game.

The pony was 'introduced' (pushed) into the charge room and the officer then switched off the light and closed the door. Pandemonium ensued inside until the door was opened again by the wag, at which the pony bolted and disappeared into the night. The joker was never identified.

Anarchists are not often found in Walsall, but this changed in 1891. A Walsall company received an order for thirty-six iron castings, but the customer's address was false and the order was not fulfilled. A couple of months later the company was told that the castings had been for bombs and six men had been arrested.

The six were all associated with Walsall Socialist Club. Some on the far left of the Socialist movement were campaigning for an end to all organised government in order to 'liberate the proletariat'. The Walsall anarchists were accused of possessing substances to cause an unlawful explosion and endanger life or property.

Police found evidence in the club and at the men's homes. Not all were locals, in fact only three were from Walsall, the others came from Norwich, France and one was an Italian living in London. One of the men said the making of the bombs was not a crime as their target was the Tsar of Russia, so they would not be used in England.

Four of the men were convicted; three received ten year sentences, one five years. An anarchist journalist, after the trial, was imprisoned for incitement to murder because he reported that the judge and the Detective Inspector in the case were 'not fit to live'.

9

RIOTS, PROTESTS
AND RISINGS

Methodist John Wesley was forcibly taken from a convert's house in October 1743. These Wednesbury riots are well known. The Darlaston mob took Wesley to the local magistrate Mr Lane at Bentley Hall who turned them away asking, 'What do I want with Wesley?' Their only allegation seemed to be that they were woken too early by hymn singing. The mob tried the same with another magistrate at Walsall, with a similar response.

The crowd then dragged Wesley back to Wednesbury. He talked all the while to his captors and some of them warmed towards him. One collier, George Clifton, carried him on his back over a stream to save him from others in the mob.

Further anti-Wesley riots took place the following February, when Methodists houses were attacked. Later Wednesbury became an important centre for the Methodists in the Black Country.

Iron-mad John Wilkinson had a thriving business, boring out cast-iron barrels for the American War of Independence. It is said that during a riot in 1790 a mob threatened to attack his Bradley Works, so he loaded up several of the twenty-four-pounder guns he had made and wheeled them into position in front of his gates. The mob sensibly retreated!

The first general strike in the Black Country took place in 1842. The widespread public unrest was regarded nationally as the first ever general strike. The result was great damage to factories and mines, as well as serious attacks on authority: magistrates houses were attacked, court records destroyed, police stations attacked, and policemen and soldiers were killed and wounded.

This was the time of the Chartists, who were initially blamed for starting the strike. However, it is thought the strike actually began in North Staffordshire. It lasted from early July until September.

Riots in April and May in Stourbridge and Dudley led to the Worcestershire Yeomanry and 3rd Dragoon Guards being deployed. The Chartist Leaders visited Oak Farm Colliery in June. Many rioters were arrested and received speedy trials at Stafford Quarter Sessions.

Many of the strikers were miners, causing fears of disorder. They were unusually restrained until 16 August when there was violence at a Halesowen Colliery, and a coal barge was swamped near Oldbury.

There was more trouble on 25 August when Oldbury miners had to be dispersed by the Yeomanry. The constable and a butty at a Tipton colliery had to run for their lives from a mob of strikers, and working miners were injured in the attack.

On 3 September two strike leaders died at Hill Top, West Bromwich, during a riot. Workers were driven from a mine so police and yeomanry arrived and the mob was driven towards Birmingham Canal.

The two fleeing strikers drowned whilst trying to escape the police. This event put an end to efforts by strikers to 'stop the pits' and miners began to drift back to work.

The women chainmakers of Cradley Heath saw a significant victory in 1910. Their work was sent around the world, yet the women were treated little better than slaves, working long hours for wages as low as $1d$ an hour.

Support came in the form of Mary Macarthur and the National Federation of Women Workers, but employers refused to pay higher wages and locked out the women. For ten weeks a fight took place; public support was sought through a proactive publicity campaign. The outcome of this activism was the first minimum wage and the eventual end to the 'sweated' trade.

There were many 'top-drawer' supporters of the campaign, including Winston Churchill, David Lloyd-George and Ramsey MacDonald from the world of politics. There were also members of the aristocracy and committed women's rights activists.

The Black Country's history is littered with examples of strikes, and the three-month long 1921 Coal Strike had a profound effect. Numerous pits were ruined because of flooding as water pumps were not in operation. Many working-class people supported the strike, despite the hardships it caused.

Miners were the most directly affected; their wages and conditions led, in part, to this bitter strike. Many small manufacturing firms were able to carry on working, but a lack of materials did affect efficiency. There was much unemployment caused by the effects of the strike which resulted in a big reduction in coal production in the region.

The Battle of St James's Schools took place in Wolverhampton in August 1933. The Wolverhampton Branch of the British Union of Fascists (BUF) held its inaugural public meeting at St James Schools in the town. Their leader was Councillor T.E. Bradley. Bradley and Mike Goulding, a national speaker for Oswald Mosley's movement, were speakers at the event.

The meeting hall was packed, but some members of the audience were Communist activists. Also present by invitation, were Birmingham BUF members. Trouble was expected so it was felt reinforcements were needed.

During the meeting there were angry exchanges of words between Bradley and the Communist elements, and as Bradley continued his oratory Fascists and Communists began fighting. The leader of the Communists was rushed and ejected from the hall.

By the end of the meeting a large excitable crowd had gathered, the police were also present in numbers. The Birmingham Fascists were escorted by police the and Wolverhampton BUF to the railway station. There were noisy scenes en route and some assaults and jostling took place.

A crowd of over 3,000, led by Communists, had followed the BUF and converged on the railway station. The police appealed for calm but the noise at the station was said to be deafening as the fearful Fascists waited for their train home. Eventually they boarded the train and left the town.

The actions of the police on the night were highly praised, and the disorder, given the numbers in attendance, could have been very much worse.

10

THE
MACABRE

In 1677, the hands of John Duncalf, it is written, rotted away after he stole a bible. The victim was Margaret Babb and the crime took place near Wolverhampton.

Duncalf was the only suspect. He swore that if he had stolen the bible he wished his hands would drop off. It was found he was a regular thief, especially of bibles, because they were easy to sell. However, Mrs Babb's bible was easy to identify.

Duncalf was challenged and gave his oath. At once he found it difficult to move his hands, which then deteriorated over a number of months, causing him eventually to confess his crime. He died soon after, but only after one John Bennet had chopped off his hands, at his request, thereby fulfilling the curse. This story was documented in 1678 by the local parson, John Illingworth.

There were two hangmen who came from Dudley, George Smith and George Incher. Most towns do not have the notoriety of having supplied one hangman, yet Dudley managed to produce two. George Smith is the better known but George Incher, born in 1825 in Porter's Field, also served.

Incher, like Smith, learnt his hangman trade whilst an inmate in Stafford Prison. In 1875 he was given the title of Chief Executioner of Staffordshire and carried out executions at Stafford, as well as at Newgate. He was a bit of a rogue; in 1877 and 1881 he appeared at the local magistrates charged with being drunk and disorderly.

Just after being made hangman Incher spent a month in gaol in Stafford for theft. On retirement, after his last execution in

February 1881, he became a drover and lived in Dudley with his family.

Abel Hill was hanged in 1820 for murdering Marie Martin. The judge who condemned him to hang also directed that his body be sent back to the scene of the crime in Bilston and for it to be publicly dissected; this was meant as a final indignity for the criminal.

This was a gruesome power given to judges up until about 1832, when the Anatomy Act of that year allowed for cadavers to be used legally for medical research. Mr Best was the surgeon appointed to carry out this macabre ruling. The skeleton was preserved and articulated, an artefact to be shown to the curious.

A Sedgley man killed his 8-year-old daughter with a poker, yet he manged to escaped the gallows. Isaac Thompson threw a poker at his daughter's head on 27 December 1862. This was the third time he had committed a dreadful crime on one of his children.

He first came to the law's attention in 1861, when he wounded another of his children. For this first offence the magistrates were sympathetic and only fined him 5s, plus costs. They also declared his wife to be 'thoroughly bad'.

At the time of the poker incident, Thompson was awaiting trial for roasting alive his 17-month-old daughter. The baby had been found dead in front of the fire, and Thompson said he had taken her downstairs to feed her and had forgotten where he had left her. An inquest found the cause of death was manslaughter and Thompson was bailed for trial. It was whilst he was on bail that he committed his third crime, when he came home from the pub and found that his wife had gone out.

Incredibly, Thompson was not prosecuted for killing his 17-month-old, and received just two weeks hard labour for killing his other daughter. It seems that blaming a 'thoroughly bad' wife counted for something of a defence in the 1860s.

Bella in the Wych Elm is a much celebrated Black Country and Worcestershire mystery. It has been talked about since the skeleton of a woman was found in the bole of a wych elm tree in Hagley Woods in 1943.

Four boys out 'bird nesting' on Lord Cobham's land made the grisly discovery. After a short delay, partly because the boys were frightened they would get into trouble, the police were informed and descended on the scene.

A police and forensic enquiry began, which ran on and off for over sixty years. Eminent forensic expert, Professor James Webster, carried out the examination of 'Bella's' remains, whilst another scientist, John Lund, examined the clothing found at the scene. The skeleton was never identified, so how did she get her name 'Bella'?

It was estimated that the body had lain in the tree for eighteen months or longer. She was about 35, had given birth and dental impressions were taken. Enquiries focused on possible suspects and missing persons, and many theories were postulated.

During the investigation, graffiti began to appear in Blackheath, Halesowen and Netherton, asking 'who put Bella in the wych elm?' Why 'Bella' and why Hagley Wood – who could she be? One theory claimed this was some kind of macabre witchcraft ritual killing; another that she was a worker, drafted in to the Black Country during the war and was not local.

A third possibility was she was part of a spy ring, possibly German or Dutch. There were also enquiries into travelling people, gypsies who may have moved on and hadn't heard of the discovery, or just hadn't missed one of their number. None of these theories have been proved or disproved.

The mystery is kept alive in the *Black Country Bugle,* though official police enquiries have now been closed. It is doubtful that the mystery will ever be solved, given the passage of time.

The case of the Great Wyrley Animal Outrages is another macabre one. It is similarly still talked about and theories are exchanged on a regular basis. It attracted the attention of Sir Arthur Conan Doyle, who turned real-life sleuth to solve the mystery and help to obtain release from prison for prime suspect George Edalji.

George was the son of Bombay-born Parsi Shapurji Edalji, who was the Anglican vicar for Great Wyrley, an isolated mining village on the northern fringe of the Black Country.

The saga began in 1903 and involved a series of attacks on horses, sheep and cows. Edalji was a Birmingham-based solicitor, to whom evidence pointed as being the perpetrator for disembowelling one horse and exposing the entrails of another. This was the eighth incident and the series baffled police and public alike.

Letters alluded to a gang being responsible for the crimes, and George was named as a member, so he became the focus of police enquiries. For some time the police had been out in force, watching for activity, but they had seen nothing.

Footprints at the scene of the latest attack led to the vicarage. The police examined clothing belonging to George, leading to his arrest the following morning at his office in Birmingham.

George was later charged on flimsy evidence. At his four-day trial he was found guilty and received a seven-year sentence. However, the maimings did not stop and further letters from the 'Wyrley Gang' were sent.

A campaign to right what was seen as a clear travesty of justice commenced. Conan Doyle began investigations that would have been a credit to Sherlock Holmes. In his view the case was exceptionally weak, and he presented evidence through a series of *Daily Telegraph* articles.

George was released on 'ticket of leave' three years into his sentence and a 1907 inquiry stated he should not have been convicted. He was allowed to continue to practice as a solicitor as a result. The case was one that eventually led to the setting up of the criminal Court of Appeal.

11

BLACK COUNTRY MURDERS

The Staffordshire Assize Roll of 1272, records one John de Chelesle chasing and catching William and Adam and accusing them of breaking into his Lord's grange at Pyshalle (Pelsall).

He bound them and then beheaded them. John was arrested for this act and taken to prison at Eccleshale. He escaped, but was quickly caught and beheaded later the same day.

In 1759 Joseph Darby and his two sons were hanged for the murder of bailiff John Walker of Witley Barn, at Colley Gate. This left Walker's children alone at the barn, which became known as 'Fatherless Barn'.

The last man to be gibbetted in the Black Country was William Howe. He was executed for the cold-blooded and callous murder of Benjamin Robins in 1812. The scene of the crime was Dunsley near Kinver; Robins was a gentleman farmer who owned Dunsley Hall. He had visited Stourbridge on business at the Saturday market in the town.

Robins was carrying just over £21 in cash and was walking home when set upon by Howe. A pistol was discharged by Howe and the ball hit Robins's spine. Howe then asked Robins to give him his money. Robins lived for ten days and gave a good description of his assailant. On request, two Bow Street runners were despatched to investigate the crime.

Howe was well known and had been seen in the vicinity of the crime. The Runners traced a pistol and bullets, then lay in wait and arrested Howe. At his trial it only took the jury 7 minutes to find him guilty. At the gallows he apparently confessed his crime.

The request for his body to be gibbeted (hung in chains) was sanctioned by the Home Secretary as deterrent to others. 40,000 people are said to have visited the gibbet the day after the body was first displayed, though I think the reporter may have added an extra '0', because it was in an isolated spot. The lane was later named because of the gibbet.

The fourth victim of Jack the Ripper was a Wolverhampton woman, the daughter of a tin plater who was born in Graisley Green. Catherine Eddowes's nickname became 'Kidney Kate', because the Ripper had removed her left kidney.

The Eddowes family moved to London when Catherine was a baby. She split from her family in 1880, having taken to drink. Catherine was the second victim of that night, Elizabeth Stride had been found murdered an hour earlier. Catherine left three children, the product of a relationship with ex-soldier Thomas Conway.

In Wolverhampton pretty young Ruth Hadley died in a tragic incident, but why? And how did her middle-class lover, Edward Lawrence, escape conviction? 29 December 1908 saw both participants in the tragedy at Edward's house, about to eat dinner.

Both had been drinking in a local pub and drank more whisky in the house, and 15-year-old Kate Maddox, a domestic help, was the last person to see both in good health. She had been there to help prepare their evening meal and stated both were under the influence, but not drunk.

Within an hour after Kate left, Edward was at a neighbour's house, a doctor, telling him: 'I have shot a woman.' Thus, one of the most intriguing cases in the Black Country began to unravel.

Despite efforts to save her, Ruth died in the hospital that same night as a result of two shots from Edward's revolver; it seemed to the police that they had a 'cut and dried' case of murder. No one else was involved and suicide was ruled out at the inquest.

Edward was quickly charged with murder. Defence Counsel was celebrated barrister Edward Marshall Hall, who initially felt that all he could achieve was a manslaughter conviction. It emerged that both Ruth and Edward were heavy drinkers and not strangers to conflict. Marshall Hall used Edward's drink problem to good effect when presenting his case, but at what cost?

Evidence was given to the jury about how Ruth was the violent one in the relationship, witnesses testified that Edward was often a victim of assault, and had been threatened with his own gun by Ruth. Edward admitted he had taken the gun from Ruth on the fateful night and fired a warning shot, which probably caused one of her wounds. Ruth got the gun back and threatened him again. There was a struggle, resulting in the fatal shot.

The balance of the case swung towards Edward being guilty only of manslaughter, or acquitted. Even the prosecutor advised the jury to convict of manslaughter. This was a bitter pill, given the prosecution's early strong case.

It was the Marshall Hall factor, using Edward's weaknesses of drink and relationship problems; he persuaded the jury that Edward was equally a victim in this incident. Edward was acquitted, but with a high cost to his reputation. His middle-class friends abandoned him, his business crumbled, he carried on drinking and faced a series of litigation cases over money.

He became bankrupt as a result, but continued to fight a stream of cases against him. Some asked how Edward managed to live in a large, well-furnished house in Kidderminster until his death in 1912. He also left £2,750 in his will, not bad for a bankrupt.

12

COURT REPORTS AND NOTABLE CRIMES

Court Reports can sometimes be amusing, but are often tragic and sad. Here is a selection of the interesting ones.

Wordsley gardener James Rodgers appeared before Brierley Hill Magistrates. PC Evans gave evidence saying 'He's always drunk'. Rodgers retorted, 'You never saw me drunk' to which PC Evans replied, 'I hardly ever saw you sober'. Rodgers was fined 5s.

A 'very small boy', Edward Hatton, was ordered to pay 8s for stealing 6d worth of straw from Levi Packwood's rick. The straw had been put around a frozen pump and set fire to thaw it out. This was before the age of criminal responsibility was established, by which no one under the age of 10 could commit a crime in law.

Two Brierley Hill women, Ellen Tracey and Harriet Williams, fought each other 'by mutual consent' in the town. A witness said they fought two rounds. The bench decided they were as bad as each other and they were fined 5s each.

One newspaper report warns of 'an embryo highwayman'. A little melodramatic for 1879? Benjamin Hughes of Buckpool was accused of stealing a small boy's cap and attempting to take his necktie.

Magistrate Mr Firmstone said this was a disgraceful act, tantamount to highway robbery, and fined him 10s or seven days.

Edward Campbell Brewer was employed by the Stourbridge Navigation Company as a clerk. He was charged with forging a bill of exchange, to the value of £13 5s on 15 August 1833, then forging an endorsement on the bill and finally disposing of the same to John Perry. This offence rendered him liable to transportation.

Brewer took flight to America and Harry Ebershard promptly set sail from Liverpool to apprehend him. Brewer was apprehended in Utica, 300 miles from New York, and brought back to England.

After hearing evidence against him at the Quarter Sessions in March 1834 the jury found Brewer 'guilty'. Brewer was to be transported for life, he raised his hands to heaven and exclaimed 'My wife, my children' (he had five young children).

Further similar charges involving over £1,000 were not proceeded with, given the conviction and sentence already secured.

In 1903 showman W.M. Cody, 'Buffalo Bill' came to Dudley with his travelling show. On one fateful afternoon he changed into his show gear and left his jewellery in a box. On returning after the show he found his jewel box had been rifled.

One significant piece stolen was a diamond pin, given to Cody at a show at Olympia by King Edward VII. Also missing were a pair of diamond cufflinks given to him in 1869 by Grand Duke Alexis Alexandrovich of Russia. In today's money it is estimated that the value of the haul was £30,000.

The culprit turned out not to be a local, but Cody's own valet, a 20-year-old Londoner. Cody's jewellery was all recovered and the thief was returned in irons to the scene of his crime, after he was convicted by Dudley Magistrates and given six months hard labour. Cody's last show in the Black Country was at Wollaston on 28 April 1904.

They say crime doesn't pay, and in the nineteenth century this was often the case. One Black Country couple were woken at 4.30 a.m. and found they had been burgled. The stolen goods were beef, pork, bread and cheese. This was reported to a constable and enquiries commenced.

Suspect Richard Bennett was visited and his house searched; beef and a marrow bone were found, which Mr Reynolds identified. Bennett said they had been given to him by his brother, but the court would have none of this and found him guilty. He was transported for ten years.

An unusual incident occurred in West Bromwich. A coachman from the town returned home with his wife and found their front door broken down. Inside, a strange dog attacked the couple. The man, John Reeves, defended himself against the dog and killed it with a poker.

In the kitchen Reeves found the burglar, John Blackham. A struggle ensued and the local constable was called, but he was not at home. Blackham was forcibly ejected from the house and lay in a stupor outside. People gathered, wondering what to do, and Blackham was taken to the workhouse but turned away. Eventually the constable came and Blackham was detained. His fate was not recorded.

13

MYSTERIES AND THINGS THAT GO BUMP!

The Black Country has had its fair share of ghostly goings on. Here is a selection of those apparitions that may or may not haunt our buildings.

Haunted historical Haden Hill House is old enough to have plenty of ghosts, with its history dating back to Tudor times. Unsurprisingly the house has been the scene for a number of deaths. If you believe in ghosts then here are a couple that may still be restlessly roaming the house.

Eleanor (or Elaine) of Hayseech Mill is said to wander, searching for her lover, a monk from Halesowen Abbey. They were planning to elope. Sadly, the legend goes, they were walled up underground in a secret passage joining the Old Hall with the Abbey. Both ghosts have been seen, he is walking round and praying, Elaine is crying and wringing her hands.

Another spirit, said to wander a path in the garden is dressed in Victorian clothing. Could be this George Alfred Haden Best? No one knows.

Wolverhampton, as a very old, established town (now a city) has its share of ghosts. It is said that a Cavalier is supposed to haunt the site of Bentley Hall, since demolished and now the site of a public library. The hall is one of the places King Charles II hid in during his escape from the Battle of Worcester in 1651.

Another ghostly Cavalier on horseback is said to haunt lanes near Northicote Farm at Bushbury, outside Wolverhampton.

Dudley Castle is one of the regions oldest buildings and has a number of ghosts. These include ghostly couples, the 'grey lady' – an elderly woman in a grey shawl, a small ghostly dog, the skeletons of two monks and a dog, hooded figures, figures around a fire and a poltergeist.

Himley is another area with its ghosts. 'The Swamp' a boggy area of Himley Plantation, is said to be haunted by a phantom horseman who could be Gideon Grove, the groom of Stephen Lyttelton, owner of Holbeche House, where some of the Gunpowder Plotters took refuge.

The house was surrounded by a posse led by Richard Walsh, Sheriff of Worcester which led to the capture or killing of those plotters. Those captured were transported to London where they were later executed.

One West Bromwich ghost is thought to be a servant girl who became trapped in a secret room at Hill House, Dagger Lane and subsequently died there.

At nearby Willenhall there is a glowing red handprint on a wall, beside the Railway Tavern, in Love Lane. It is said to be the blood stained hand of PC Enoch Augustus Hooper, stabbed to death on 8 December 1865 when in pursuit of an offender involved in a disturbance at the Royal George Inn, Walsall Street.

Hooper had gone to the assistance of another officer. Husband and wife Patrick and Mary Cain were arrested for the crime and tried at Stafford. They were both acquitted. No one else was ever prosecuted for the murder, which may be why the ghostly hand remains.

Not a ghost story, but a folk legend was Pelsall's 'fiery horse'. Some older residents may still remember being told the tale of a farmer who had a horse with lice. He treated it by using a paraffin rub.

One night the horse became restless and the farmer went to investigate the cause, carrying a candle for light.

It is said the fumes from the paraffin ignited and the horse bolted, startling a group of miners on their way to a night shift. They reported seeing the devil riding a horse with the flames of hell around him.

Black Country miners were a superstitious lot. They believed that anything stolen from a dead colleague would mean the spirit of the dead miner would haunt the pit until the property was restored.

Hell Lane in Sedgley was described as the 'most unruly place' in the Black Country. Its moniker applied from the eighteenth to the early twentieth century. A woman who lived in the lane (now renamed Ettingshall Lane) was said to have been a witch and could turn herself into a white rabbit to spy on her neighbours.

There was also a Hell Hole at Lye, a Hell Bank near Stourbridge and other examples from further afield. One suggestion is that the Lye version of Hell was actually Cradley Forge, probably a hellish place to work.

Warding off evil spirits was high on some Black Country people's priorities in days of yore. A Bradley man said he always wore a strand from the noose that hanged Abel Hill at Stafford in 1820. He said this would protect him from witches.

Hill killed his partner, Mary Martin, who was pregnant with a child Hill didn't want. He tried medicine to induce a miscarriage, which failed. He also killed their young son, Thomas. Both Mary and Thomas went missing and eight days later their bodies were found in the local canal at Bilston. Hill believed he would be acquitted, but a jury quickly found him guilty, and he was hanged.

It was a regular practice for hangmen to cut up the rope from an execution and sell it on. In celebrated cases the hangman could make a guinea an inch for the rope.

Dragon-lore may be popular today because of films and TV shows, but in eighteenth- and nineteenth-century Black Country folk lore they do not feature much (perhaps because many people worked underground). Except ...

> The dragon of Wednesbury churches ate
> (he used to come on Sunday)
> Whole congregations were to him
> A dish of salmagundi*
> The corporation worshipful
> He valued not an ace
> But swallowed the Mayor, asleep in his chair
> And picked his teeth with the mace

*Salmagundi was a seventeenth-century English salad dish, with meats, seafood, vegetable, fruit, flowers, nuts and leaves, with oil and vinegar dressing.

You will not be surprised to hear that records of Wednesbury mayors do not include one who met his demise in this manner.

Just who is AJW, the mysterious Mario Lanza ghostwriter? For fifty years someone has been leaving 'calling cards' with a hand-drawn picture of the Philadelphia-born, American tenor with a variety of messages. They have been left in pubs, shops (especially charity shops) and plenty of other places as well.

They are mainly drawn on Bathams beer mats and it is estimated that about 250,000 have been left. These are mainly in the Black Country, but also further afield in England, as well as a few in Spain and the Caribbean, posted to selected 'victims' in England. Some are thought to have been left by a helper, especially the overseas cards.

AJW was interviewed on TV by John Swallow many years ago (he wore a mask). A documentary has recently been filmed outlining his exploits and trying, albeit in a light-hearted way, to track him down; a bit like the *Pink Panther* meets the *Phantom of the Opera*!

Some people know the secret, but they will not tell. Exposure would be a tragedy for AJW and the Black Country.

His work has been featured in an exhibition at the Public in West Bromwich, and I have previously described his work as 'non-destructive graffiti'.

I have been targeted by AJW, with cards and collages arriving through the post. I also interviewed AJW for the aforementioned documentary, but he again wore a mask. He was the genuine article and I watched him draw one of his trade mark cards before my eyes. All in all a fascinating tale and a real Black Country legend.

14

WHETHER
THE WEATHER

1946–47 saw a cruel winter in the Black Country. This was the year immediately after the end of the Second World War, industry was re-adjusting from making material for the war and the armed forces were being demobilised. The country was almost bankrupt because of the war. What else could go wrong?

What about the worst winter for over 130 years! In late January 1947 bitterly cold easterly winds began to blow across the country. There followed three days of snow showers, and then on 27 January a blizzard hit the Black Country, blocking roads and causing great difficulties for travellers. More snow followed and people worried about their coal supplies.

As January blew out, February announced its arrival. The 2nd signalled the shape of things to come; three days of snow left a depth of around 14ins (36cm). The *Express and Star* reported 17ft drifts and mines had to close, leading to coal shortages; workers across the region were left idle. Snow clearance was a priority, with even Prisoners of War being used in the effort.

There was another 10ins (26cm) of snow fall in some areas on 8 February. The roof of a factory in Alma Street, Smethwick, collapsed under the weight of 9ft of snow from the latest blizzard. Later in the month more snow fell, closing more roads, and the struggle to keep roads open was constantly hampered by persistent strong winds.

February turned into March, but there was no end to the cold and snow. The 4th and 5th saw the worst blizzard of the winter so far, adding up to a further 2ft (60cm). One unusual problem was the escape of seven wolves from their enclosure at Dudley Zoo. Five were shot to prevent them from escaping from the grounds due to the fear that their hunger would make them dangerous.

The end finally came on 16 March, with 5 hours of howling gales causing damage to buildings and trees. The *Dudley Herald* newspaper recorded 100mph gusts of wind. Problems still had to be overcome, warmer Atlantic air brought in milder weather, but heavy rain as well. Inevitably rivers flooded; the worst in living memory.

It has been said that Dudley is a 'top-coat colder than Stourbridge'. A *Daily Mirror* cartoonist once drew a cartoon depicting a Scottish Highlander cutting his own throat. At the time the recipient lived on a ridge called Highland Road, Shavers End, on Brierley Hill. The Dudley wind is often still described as a 'lazy wind' as it doesn't bother to go round you, but straight through!

The Dudley earthquake in 2002 measured five on the Richter Scale and lasted for 20 seconds. Its epicentre was at the junction of Himley Road and High Arcal Road. The tremor was felt as far away as North Yorkshire and London.

I was working nights in Birmingham and felt the tremor. It woke my wife in Halesowen and she rang me in a panic, thinking she was being burgled! There are plenty of other personal tales of those shaken awake.

One casualty of the earthquake was St John's Church in Kates Hill. This was badly damaged and condemned. A preservation group was set up to try and save it and it is hoped that it will be able to reopen soon. The church is home to the grave of the Tipton Slasher and many other notable locals.

15

BLACK COUNTRY PEOPLE

Employers often say their people are the most important asset. The same can be said for our fine and upstanding citizens in the Black Country. Also, without some of our shadier characters life would not have been so rich or colourful. So here is a short selection.

PHILANTHROPY AND THE GOOD

John Corbett became known as the Salt King. He was one of the most famous Black Country industrialists and philanthropists. In 1852 Corbett moved from The Delph, Brierley Hill to Stoke Prior at Droitwich, with an eye on setting up a career in salt.

Corbett was determined and stubborn about making his business a success, though others in the salt business thought he was mad or a fool. He proved his detractors wrong and beat them on their home ground. Corbett introduced new technology, producing 3,000 tons of salt every week, rightly earning his 'Salt King' title.

Corbett was also a good employer and respected by his workers. He improved conditions and segregated the male and female workers to improve their morals (he was a strong supporter of womens' rights and later an advocate of womens' suffrage). He provided workers with good housing, a school and dispensary.

Corbett also built a real French Chateau called Impney just outside Droitwich, but why? In 1855 he went on a trip to Paris.

Here he met and later married Anna Eliza O'Meara, whose father was Secretary of the Diplomatic Corps in the city.

In 1868 Corbett commissioned the building of Chateau Impney. In 1875 the Corbett family moved in, by now with four children, and Anna took an instant dislike to the building. Four years later, following Anna's friendship with a local priest, the couple separated.

Corbett died in 1901, aged 83. In 1906 the Impney furniture and effects were disposed of, later his properties were also sold, including Impney. The chateau passed through a number of hands over the years.

During the Second World War it became an interrogation centre for the Americans, and the British Army used parts of the estate to experiment with poisonous gas. After the war the dilapidated Chateau was bought and restored in 1945.

In 1947 it opened as a luxurious hotel and night club. In 1963 it became a disco and casino and finally in 1970 it became a sixty-six-bedroom luxury hotel. Since then it has had a number of owners, but remains a hotel and is an iconic building in the heart of Worcestershire.

Dorothy Wyndlow Pattison is much better known as Sister Dora and also as the Florence Nightingale of Walsall. After school in Yorkshire she joined the Sisterhood of the Good Samaritan and became Sister Dora.

She arrived in Walsall in 1865 to work at the cottage hospital, replacing a sick colleague. She is a true legend, best known for her devotion to duty and nursing abilities. Examples of her devotion include tending to eleven seriously injured burn victims from a blast at an ironworks and her sympathetic care given to the bereaved of a mining disaster that killed twenty-two men entombed underground.

An example of Dora's devotion came when smallpox visited the town for the second time in 1875. Dora volunteered to go to the isolation hospital to give people confidence in her and encourage others to visit relatives. For six months she lived in at the hospital, nursing victims of the epidemic, until it died out.

When she developed breast cancer she kept it secret from everyone, including her doctor. She died on Christmas Eve in

1878, aged 66. Even when diagnosed with cancer she carried on caring for people until confined to bed, and even then she continued directing hospital affairs.

A newspaper tribute to her read: 'We worship her memory as the most saintly thing that was ever given to us. Her name is immortalised both by her own surpassing goodness and by the love of a whole people for her.'

Kingswinford-born John Addenbrooke was one of the 'Good'. He was a medical doctor, also a fellow and bursar at Catharine Hall, now St Catharine's College in Cambridge. In 1719 he became the first Englishmen to bequeath his wealth of more than £4,500 to fund a voluntary hospital: Addenbrooke's at Cambridge.

Edward Henry Lane Noott was the first vicar of the parish of St John's in Kates Hill. He spent sixty-two years in that position, unprecedented in the Black Country and possibly a record for the Anglican Church.

Noott was born in Cardigan, studied at Corpus Christi College at Cambridge and was initially curate at the Parish Church in Tipton. In 1847 he married Sarah Haden Hickman, daughter of Sir Alfred Hickman, who founded Tarmac and was a Wolverhampton MP. Noott died in 1905.

General William Booth, founder of the Salvation Army, lived at No. 5 Hatherton Street in Walsall during the 1860s. He ran a mission in the town, and worked to build a Revival Chapel mission hall in Bloxwich, which later became Revival Street.

In 1865 the Booth family moved to Whitechapel, London, where the Salvation Army evolved. Booth came back to the Black Country in 1904, as part of a motor tour from Land's End to Aberdeen. He passed through Brierley Hill en route to speak in Dudley. Again in 1909 he was photographed driving through Wall Heath as part of a country-wide campaign tour.

John Wesley made many visits to the Black Country, Wednesbury in particular. He was much loved, but in his early days there were also riots against his activities, covered elsewhere in this book.

Wesley taught the value of 'The Method' of Methodism and found many converts. Local congregations were fiercely loyal and there are many examples of Wesleyan Methodist Chapels around the Black Country.

PROMINENT PERSONALITIES

John Dudley was the 23rd Baron of Dudley. He became a very powerful man in England, a first-class athlete and talented jouster. In 1543 John was created High Admiral to Henry VIII.

In 1545 John had to command a fleet of forty warships against a French armada, which sailed in the Solent. This was the battle in which the *Mary Rose* was sunk. The French were able to land on the Isle of Wight, but withdrew a few days later. The French fleet was later defeated off Shoreham and was a costly fiasco for them.

William Bourne became one of the most prolific nineteenth-century church and civic building designers in the Black Country. The Bourne family were significant in the Dudley area for several generations, with five being Mayors of Dudley between 1776 and 1837.

St John's Church at Kates Hill was one of William's projects around the region (which also included St James Church School) and has been moved to the Black Country Living Museum. Other projects included the second Dudley Town Hall, Dudley Guest Hospital (including the lodge) and the Mechanics Institute in Dudley.

Sir Mervyn King was the 118th Governor of the Bank of England and retired from the job in June 2013. He was born in 1948 at Chesham Bois, Buckinghamshire and his family moved to Wolverhampton when he was a young boy. He grew up in Wolverhampton and attended Wolverhampton Grammar School.

The case of Fiddler Foley and early industrial espionage is an interesting one. Richard Foley was a successful producer of iron and introduced the slitting mill to the Black Country. Legend has it he went to Sweden, via Hull, and wore beggar's clothes, to learn the secret of slitting.

Foley played a violin while dancing along the road, all the time heading for the iron works. He is said to have charmed the secret of the slitting mill with his actions and returned home.

Unfortunately, the first visit left him with a mill that failed to work properly, so he repeated his journey and completed his knowledge, returning to build a fully-functioning slitting mill. A similar tale has the espionage taking place in Holland, but still mentions two visits to get the job done properly.

William Caslon was born in 1692 at Cradley. He was a gunsmith, but became famous for designing some of the first typefaces for printing. They became very popular and some of his designs are still in use today, though these days we would refer to them as fonts. The first printed version of the United States Declaration of Independence used a Caslon typeface.

NOTABLE OUTSIDERS

In the late 1800s Sir Edward Elgar was a regular visitor to the Rectory of St Peter's in Waterloo Road, Wolverhampton, next to the Molineux. Elgar became a Wolverhampton Wanderers fan. He also attended horse racing at Dunstall Park on at least one occasion.

Sir Arthur Conan-Doyle, the creator of Sherlock Holmes and a qualified doctor, came to the Black Country on several occasions. Between 1878 and 1881, during his studies, Conan Doyle worked in Aston, Birmingham. Obviously this does not count as a visit to the Black Country, but it is a 'near miss'.

In 1893 Conan Doyle did come to the Black Country on invitation, as a public speaker to lecture to Walsall Literary Institutes on the subject of 'Facts about Fiction'. A few years later Conan Doyle returned to the Walsall/Bloxwich area to turn detective himself, when he became intimately involved in the case of George Edalji.

One more obtuse link for Conan Doyle was that one of his fictional heroines was described as 'head of a private school at Walsall'. Miss Violet Hunter was the heroine in 'The Adventure of the Copper Beeches', published in 1892.

In May 1911 Sir Robert Baden Powell reviewed the Stourbridge and District Boy Scouts on a visit to the town. Before coming to Stourbridge he inspected the Scouts at Halesowen and went on to Kidderminster after leaving Stourbridge. The Stourbridge review took place in the grounds of Oldwinsford Hospital.

Labour leader Keir Hardie came to speak at Stourbridge Town Hall in 1913. Hardie was the first member of the Independent Labour Party to be elected to the House of Commons. He was first elected in 1892, lost his seat in 1895, but was re-elected in 1900. Hardie was a supporter of women's suffrage and this formed part of his talk.

THE INFAMOUS AND NOTORIOUS

The 'Notorious' Reverend William Moreton seems a bit of an odd title – notorious is not necessarily a word you want to hear when describing a 'man of the cloth', but it was wholly appropriate for Moreton.

William was appointed curate to Willenhall and Darlaston churches in 1786. His sins would soon surface for all to see. He enjoyed gambling, drink and cruel sports and also kept bad company. In 1791 Moreton was fined for sporting with a gun and two setting dogs. However, he was allegedly popular with the 'lower order'.

Moreton's bizarre behaviour included regularly conducting services sitting, as he was too drunk to stand. Moreton once stopped the bishop's coach in Willenhall and offered him a tankard of ale. He also used un-clergyman-like language in church, where could he be very aggressive

Moreton died in 1834, leaving heavy debts. His memory has been preserved by a number of small statues created in his image, some of which are still in existence. A poem was written about the exploits of the notorious reverend:

A tumbledown church
A tottering steeple
A drunken parson
And a wicked people

Neville George Clevely Heath was not as clever as his name suggests. He impersonated the Earl of Dudley (William Dudley Ward) to carry out a con. In his defence, he did resemble the Earl. Heath was later executed for the murders of Margery Gardner and Doreen Marshall in London and Bournemouth.

Jonathan Wild was a notorious Wolverhampton robber. He was born in Walsall Street in the town in about 1682. He was famed for his criminality in the eighteenth century, but his story also illustrates the failings within the criminal justice system of the day.

Wild abandoned his wife to live in London. He lived in a brothel in Covent Garden and learned to pickpocket, using an accomplice to distract victims. He also became a thief taker and negotiated the return of stolen goods, often sending thieves to gaol or to the gallows.

He set up an office near the Old Bailey, where he controlled a network of thieves and informers. He used his role as a receiver of stolen goods and taker of thieves to claim high rewards for the return of property.

Wild became wealthy, but he worried the government; he helped control criminality, but his darker dealings were alarming. In 1725 Wild was accused of stealing £50 of lace and receiving £10 for its return. He was found guilty of a new law that prohibited the receiving of a reward and sentenced to hang. He appealed to the king for clemency, but to no avail.

The night before his hanging he tried to commit suicide by taking laudanum, but only made himself semi-conscious. Wild was hanged and his body smuggled away, ending up in a museum in the Royal College of Surgeons.

A notorious highwayman terrorised parts of the Black Country in the 1750s. 'Rowley Jack' was his moniker and he did much of his 'work' between Whiteheath and Dudley. The terrain was wild and hilly (still is – well, hilly anyway).

Abraham Fox was the Whiteheath blacksmith. His forge was also a beer house, which had accommodation for overnight guests. It became a stopping place for the stagecoaches, the main public transport of the day. This was the area where many of Jack's victims passed through. He was described as being dressed like a gentleman, and was armed with a pistol and a sword.

A number of efforts were made to capture Jack, but all met with failure, the trail often dying out on the outskirts of Tividale. One night, surveillance revealed a mystery horseman arriving at the blacksmith's house, where he was met by the daughter of Abraham Fox, Rebecca. The pair were challenged and they burst out of the stable on a single horse.

The couple were chased for miles before the hunt was abandoned. However, this was the last contact anyone had with Jack or Rebecca. Some years later the mystery was finally solved with the discovery of two skeletons in a secret underground vault, beneath Brinfield Hall in Tividale.

An examination of the clothing worn, and the presence of the skeleton of a horse, made it almost conclusive that this was Jack and Rebecca. The hooves of the horse even matched hoof prints left when Jack had been active.

Alice Grey was an infamous Wolverhampton fraudster. She reported having had her purse stolen in several towns by boy purse-snatchers in order to receive alms from town officials. She was eventually tried for perjury at Stafford in 1855.

John Stonehouse was first elected as Labour MP for Wednesbury in 1957. He became a Minister and Privy Councillor during his career, and was also Postmaster General. In 1974 he became Walsall North MP. However, Stonehouse will not only be remembered for his contribution to politics.

In 1974 Stonehouse faked his own death by leaving his clothes on a beach in Miami. He was later found and arrested in Australia on Christmas Eve of that year. He was tried in 1976 for charges including fraud, theft, forgery and conspiracy to defraud, Stonehouse was found guilty and sentenced to seven years' imprisonment.

Stonehouse resigned the Labour whip, which made them a minority government. The subsequent by-election was won by a Conservative, Robin Hodgson. Stonehouse died in 1988, aged 62. Recently it was publicly revealed that Stonehouse had been an agent for the communist Czechoslovak Socialist Republic military intelligence.

ENTERTAINERS FROM THE BLACK COUNTRY

The Black Country has been the birthplace of a number of world-famous entertainers. Taking aside the sports men and women, who will be covered elsewhere, here are some of the actors, actresses, singers and comedians who have entertained beyond the borders of our region.

Dame Maggie Teyte, prima donna, was born in Wolverhampton in 1888. She was one of the world's best-loved opera singers. Her first public appearance was in Paris in 1906. She changed her name from 'Tate' to 'Teyte' because the French regularly mispronounced her surname.

Maggie's final concert appearance was at the Royal Festival Hall in 1956. When she died, aged 88, it was said that she was a sad figure and nearly bankrupt.

Black Country actor and director James Whale was born in 1889 at Kates Hill, Dudley. His father was a blast furnace man and James was schooled in Dudley and initially worked at a cobbler's shop. He then moved on to work at Harper and Bean. He behaved and looked like a gentleman.

James showed early artistic inclination and enrolled as an evening student at Dudley School of Arts. Before the First World War there is no evidence of him having been on stage, but his artistic ability was emerging. Whale took a commission in the Worcestershire Regiment, but only reluctantly.

In 1917 Whale was captured by the Germans in Belgium. During his captivity he did hundreds of line and wash drawings, many of which he later sold.

Once back in England he joined Birmingham Repertory Company. In 1923 he moved to London and found work as an actor, producer and set designer. In 1928 his career was transformed. Whale took on the production of a new play *Journey's End* by R.C. Sherriff. The lead was played by Laurence Olivier.

The play was snapped up by the Savoy Theatre and ran for over twelve months, mostly without Olivier who left to make the film *Beau Geste*. Whale then went to America with the play and directed the film version. He went on to work with Boris Karloff and later with Charles Laughton and Raymond Massey. In the early 1940s Whale left the film industry and returned to painting, aged 52. He died in 1957 at his home in California.

Chriss Gittins is probably best known as Walter Gabriel from *The Archers*. He was born in 1902 at West Street in Stourbridge and was christened Chriss. This was not a typing or recording error; his father wanted him to be a Chris rather than Christopher, but the registrar protested that this was not a 'proper' name.

After debate there was a compromise and the second 's' was added. Chriss first acted in *The Archers* as Walter Gabriel in 1953, but had played 'bit-parts' in the series before taking on his most famous role. He also worked in television and was the subject of a *This is Your Life* episode in 1984.

Richard Wattis was a Wednesbury born actor and comedian. He appeared in *Carry On* films, *St Trinians* and several Norman Wisdom films. With trademark thick-rimmed glasses, he was often portrayed in 'man from the ministry' parts. He died of a heart attack in a London restaurant in 1975, aged 62.

Bill Oddie was born in Rochdale but educated at Halesowen Grammar School. He was on TV from 1964 in

The Braden Beat with Bernard Braden, on radio in *I'm Sorry I'll Read that Again* from 1965, but best-known for comedy show *The Goodies*. In 2001 Bill was the third person to turn down the red book of *This is Your Life*, but he quickly reconsidered and accepted.

Nowadays Bill is best known for his natural history work. His first article appeared in the *West Midland Bird Club Annual* in 1962. He was made OBE in 2003 and has also been honoured by various conservation and naturalist organisations.

Sue Lawley was born in Sedgley in 1946 and educated at Dudley Girls High School. Whilst at University in Bristol she was persuaded to lose her Black Country accent. Sue began as a reporter, and in 1972 was appearing regularly on *Nationwide*, the BBC TV news programme.

Next Sue became a presenter on *Tonight* as one of the anchors. She also presented *Desert Island Discs* from 1988 to 2006. Since 2006 Sue has largely been out of the public eye, though she still makes occasional TV appearances.

Robert Plant was born in West Bromwich in 1948 and grew up in Halesowen. He became lead singer of rock band Led Zeppelin. His music career spans over forty years and he has been named as 'The greatest voice in rock'. He worked for a time in Woolworths in Halesowen, but then began his rise as a rock musician.

Robert was a member of Band of Joy with the late John Bonham and then joined Jimmy Page in The Yardbirds, which then led to the formation of Led Zeppelin. The band broke up in 1980 and Plant has had a very successful solo career ever since.

Phil Lynott is another famous West Bromwich born musician. He was born at Hallam Hospital (now Sandwell General) in 1950. He formed the group Thin Lizzy in 1970. His song 'Yellow Pearl' became the *Top of The Pops* theme tune. Phil's mother was Irish and his father Afro-Guyanese. He grew up in Dublin and was musical from an early age. He died in 1986 of pneumonia and heart failure.

Julie Walters was born in Smethwick in 1950 and educated at Holly Lodge. Her early jobs include selling insurance and being a nurse at the Queen Elizabeth hospital in Birmingham. She said the worst job for her in nursing was testing people's stools!

Julie left nursing to study English and Drama at Manchester Polytechnic. Her early work was with Victoria Wood, and she was best-known for the character Mrs Overall in *Victoria Wood as Seen on TV*. She was also half of the *Wood and Walters* TV show in 1982.

Julie has had a wide film career. In the 1980s she starred in films such as *Educating Rita* and *Buster*, and was also in the stage version of *Educating Rita*. Later Julie starred in seven of the eight *Harry Potter* films, where she played Molly Weasley.

Julie is married to former AA patrolman Grant, and the couple have a daughter, Maisie, born in 1988. She says of the future: 'I think of doing my washing so I've something to wear tomorrow'. Julie was made OBE in 1999 and CBE in 2008.

Janice Nicholls coined the phrase 'Oi'll give it foive'. She was born in Wednesbury in the 1950s and used her Black Country dialect to good effect. Her catchphrase was synonymous with sixties TV programme *Thank Your Lucky Stars*, on which she appeared regularly. After being dropped from the show in 1965, Janice trained as a chiropodist and set up a surgery in Hednesford.

Stand-up comic Frank Skinner was born at Hallam Hospital in 1957 and christened Christopher Graham Collins. This was not seen as a suitable name for a comedian and Frank experimented with 'Wes Bromwich' before settling on Frank Skinner as his stage name.

Frank's father was a semi-professional footballer, who met his mother while playing against WBA in an FA Cup game in 1937. Frank is a lifelong 'Baggie' and regularly attends matches. He has a son, born in 2012, with his long-term girlfriend Cath Mason.

Frank's early career was tough. In the day he was lecturing at Halesowen College, running comedy workshops, at night he worked as a stand-up comedian, largely unpaid. His break came in 1991 when he won the Perrier Award at the Edinburgh Festival.

His TV debut came in 1992 on Central Weekend, where his performance led to 131 complaints, including one from MP Edwina Currie. Since then he has been a TV regular, with series *Fantasy Football League* and *The Frank Skinner Show*, but some material was too risqué for the 1990s BBC. Frank also turned his attention to writing for TV, including *Room 101* and 1990s series *Blue Heaven*.

Dudley comedian and actor Lenny Henry was born in 1958 at Burton Road Hospital and was educated at the Blue Coat School. His TV career began in 1975 when he won 'New Faces' – his success was down to an impression of Stevie Wonder.

Lenny was co-presenter on Saturday morning children's show *TISWAS* from 1978 to 1981. After meeting Dawn French he was persuaded to move over to the alternative comedy scene as a stand-up and character comedian.

Lenny's BBC TV show *The Lenny Henry Show* began in 1984, where he developed some of his famous characters. Lenny then turned his talents to the big screen, drama and as a chef in a comedy series. He also tried his hand at soul singing.

In the twenty-first century Lenny has also appeared on stage, with roles in *Othello* and the *Comedy of Errors*. He is a truly all-round entertainer, and still finds time to be involved with the charity 'Comic Relief' and manages to retain his strong Black Country roots.

LOCAL ENTERTAINERS

Dolly Allen was the undisputed Queen of Black Country comedy, best known for her deadpan delivery. Dolly was a member of the original 'Black Country Night Out' for over twenty years and helped to raise thousands of pounds for charity.

Dolly was born at Wordsley Workhouse in 1906 and was orphaned ten days later. She was adopted and grew up at No. 78 Stourbridge Road, Halesowen. Her first job was at the nearby Grove's Button Factory.

In 1926 Dolly married Leonard James Allen. She began making appearances at clubs in the Halesowen area during the Second World War and appeared on radio in 1956 with Bill Maynard. In 1968 Dolly won the Black Country dialect competition at Dudley Festival.

She had TV and radio appearances in the 1970s and the Black Country Night Out toured Spain and Canada. Dolly's catchphrase was 'Hello my luvvers'. She died in 1990 after a short illness.

Tommy Mundon is another Halesowen comedian and he still lives in the town. He was another stalwart of the Black Country Night Out. Tom gave his first public appearance at the age of 5 or 6, telling a story about a pig who had been raised on ''um med baircon'.

Tom's Junior School was the County Modern Boys School, now Windsor High. He left school at 15 and worked at Blackheath Co-op. He later worked for Dudley Council and was a familiar sight driving his lorry around Halesowen, waving at his many fans as he drove.

Tom officially began his career in comedy aged 15, at a chapel concert party, when he dressed as a tramp. He performed until he was 78, when he officially retired. During his career he appeared on BBC TV's *Off the Cuff* show and also made regular radio appearances.

Aynuck and Ayli are legends on the Black Country comedy scene. Their names are a derivation of Enoch and Eli, which originated in the late nineteenth century music hall, with comedian Ernie Garner. The live birth of the Black Country duo came about over forty years ago.

Ayli has been characterised throughout by Alan Smith, and Aynuck has had three incarnations during his time. The last was John Plant, who was Aynuck for twenty years. Sadly John died in 2006 and has not been replaced. His headstone bears the legend 'Forever Remembered as Ayli'.

Aynuck and Ayli never researched their material, preferring a more off-the-cuff style, developing a subject as they went. The duo, in all their guises, played on the image of a pair of

'ERE'S FRED, E'S JED'

stereotypical Black Country men with cloth caps. They played on the dialect of the area to great effect.

The duo was once employed to help overseas medical staff get accustomed to the Black Country accent.

Well-known and highly respected Black Country comedian Harry Harrison sadly died in 2007. A great exponent of the dialect, 'Arry both wrote and spoke in dialect. His worth was recognised in 2012 with a blue plaque, which has been sited on the wall at Bloomfield Street Community Centre, Tipton. This is a spit and a throw from where 'Arry was born in 1922, Bloomfield Road.

Danny Cannon and the Ramrods were arguably Bilston's greatest rock and roll group in the late 1950s. They were all pupils of Etheridge Secondary Modern School in Bilston: Danny Robinson, Ken Hooper, Alan Lacey, Len Beddow, Pete and Walton.

Danny became the singer because he had invested in the group's microphone. Len bought the guitar and Alan Lacey purchased the drum. Pete elected to play bass and Ken became rhythm guitarist.

In 1965 they changed their name to Herbie's People.

They were very popular throughout the greater Midlands area. In Bilston the lads played regularly at Saturday night dances in the Town Hall and enjoyed a huge and loyal following.

'The Plazents' were a group that almost made the charts in 1964. Their name derived from the Plaza Ballroom in Old Hill, where they were the resident act. They were partly Birmingham and partly Black Country band, and later became the more well-known outfit The Brumbeats.

Their style was similar to the 'Mersey Beat' bands, which promoters mimicked by using the 'Brum Beat' term. The band members went their own ways after about a year.

BLACK COUNTRY AUTHORS

There is a rich seam of writers who can be associated with the Black Country. Some have achieved national and international success, others may only be known in the Black Country.

The list of Black Country Writers (not exhaustive):
Samuel Johnson (1709–1784) a 'man of letters' who attended King Edward VI School Stourbridge in 1724
William Shenstone (1714–1763) poet from Halesowen, lived at The Leasowes
John Darwell (1731–1789) poet and hymn writer from Walsall
Mary Darwell (1738–1825) (wife of John) poet from Walsall
Thomas Moss (1740–1808) poet from Brierley Hill
John Cornfield (1820–1890) poet from Coseley

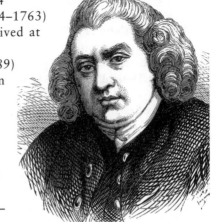

David Christie Murray (1847–1907) journalist and novelist from West Bromwich

Jerome Klapka Jerome (1859–1927) humanist from Walsall

Ellen Thorneycroft Fowler (1860–1929) novelist from Wolverhampton

Henry Newbolt (1862–1938) poet from Bilston

Edith Henrietta Fowler (1864–1944) (sister of Ellen) novelist from Wolverhampton

Evelyn Underhill (1875–1941) mystic from Wolverhampton

Alfred Noyes (1880–1958) poet from Wolverhampton

Francis Brett Young (1884–1954) novelist from Halesowen

Hugh Walters (1910–1993) science-fiction from Bilston

Henry Treece (1911–1966) poet and children's historical novelist from Wednesbury

Ian Serraillier (1912–1994) novelist, taught at Dudley Grammar School between 1939 and 1946

Kenneth Bird (1916–1993) journalist, dramatist and thriller writer from Wolverhampton

Meg Hutchinson (Born 1933) romantic novelist from Wednesbury

Michael Taylor (Born 1942) romantic novelist from Dudley

Judith Cutler (Born 1946) novelist from Oldbury

Archie Hill (pre-1939–1989) author

Allan Ahlberg (Born 1938) children's author from Oldbury

Bob Bibby (Born 1942) crime novelist and travel writer from Wolverhampton

Michael Dibdin (1947–2007) crime novelist (Aurelis Zen) from Wolverhampton

Len Webster (Born 1948) poet and novelist from Smethwick

Paul McDonald (Born 1961) author from Walsall

Francis Brett Young was born in Halesowen in 1884 and wrote a series of well-researched novels set in Birmingham, the Black Country and the region's green borderlands in the nineteenth and early twentieth centuries.

Within the Black Country he explores Wednesford and Wolverbury (Wednesbury and Wolverhampton), Sedgebury and Halesby (Sedgley and Halesowen) and Dulston (Dudley).

Young was a prolific writer, producing music, poetry, plays, short stories, non-fiction and novels, twelve of which: *The Iron Age* (1916), *The Young Physician* (1919), *The Black Diamond* (1921), *Cold Harbour* (1924), *Portrait of Clare* (1927), *My Brother Jonathan* (1928), *Mr & Mrs Pennington* (1931), *White Ladies* (1935), *Far Forest* (1936), *They Seek a Country* (1937), *Dr Bradley Remembers* (1938) and *Wistanslow* (1956) have Black Country settings. A flavour of these settings comes from *Cold Harbour*:

> A landscape that took our breath away: the whole basin of the Black Country, with innumerable smoke-stacks rising out of it like the merchant shipping of the world laid up in an estuary at low tide, each chimney flying a great pennant of smoke that blew away on the wind, and the whole scene bleared by the light of a sulphurous sunset. It was like the landscape of the end of the world.

Jerome Klapka Jerome is the Walsall author best known for his work *Three Men in a Boat*. Most of his literary work was done in London as the Jerome family moved out of Walsall to Stourbridge when he was 2 years old and thence to London. However, he was honoured with the Freedom of the Borough in 1927.

His birthplace on Caldmore Road was renamed 'Belsize House' after his death in June 1928. His last home was in Belsize Park in London. The house is now home to the Jerome K. Jerome Museum.

The BBC used *Three Men in a Boat* as inspiration for a TV programme where Dara Ó Briain, Rory McGrath and Griff Rhys Jones repeated the journey in 2006. The show was so popular the three went on a further six similar journeys, taking in places such as Ireland and New England.

David Christie Murray wrote *A Capful O' Nails*, about the harsh realities of working life in the industrial Black Country. He was particularly sympathetic toward the nailers. The book was first published in 1896 and has been re-printed a number of times. It tells the story of a nail maker who stood up for fellow workers against the foggers, who used underhanded methods to avoid paying the proper rate for workers' nails.

The book is a novel, but also a documentary and an indictment of the nail trade in the 1890s. Murray was born in West Bromwich in 1847 and was a journalist and war correspondent. He died in 1907 and is remembered with a memorial tablet in West Bromwich Central Library.

Archie Hill was a Black Country author who was hugely talented. He was 'very rough Black Country' with a lived-in face. An alcoholic with suicidal tendencies, he was said to be programmed to self-destruct, but always had a smile and a twinkle in his eye.

Hill's *Cage of Shadows* described the nine months he spent in Stafford Mental Hospital and the book became a best seller. Archie was a hard worker; he wrote radio talks and BBC scripts, including episodes of *Z-Cars*. Though his books are long out of print now, some were translated into nine languages.

Archie wrote about real people and real life. His last work *An Empty Glass* was published in 1984. Sadly, he killed himself in 1989.

Michael Dibdin was born in Wolverhampton in 1947, but brought up in Lisburn, Northern Ireland. He wrote the *Aurelio Zen* series of books about a fictional Italian detective. He wrote eleven books in all, his last, written in 2007, was published posthumously. Michael died in Seattle, Washington after a short illness.

BLACK COUNTRY POETS

James Woodhouse was an early eighteenth-century poet from Portway, Rowley Regis. He was an odd character, a shoemaker as a boy, and a friend of William Shenstone who used to lend him books. He was known by the London public as 'The shoemaker poet' and was a curiosity to them.

Woodhouse was not a great poet, but lived long and wrote much, most of it mediocre.

Halesowen poet William Shenstone was born at The Leasowes, Halesowen in 1714. He loved books from an early age and was schooled at Solihull Grammar School. There he became competent in Latin and Greek and began writing his own verse after his education finished.

William also became interested in landscaped gardening. When he took up residence at The Leasowes he turned a marl-pit into a grotto and built a 'hermitage' using stone from the Halesowen Abbey ruins. These were only two of his gardening exploits.

Shenstone mixed in high circles, but didn't have their wealth. He fell into debt, which made him feel wretched. Possibly because of this he was sympathetic towards the poor, including a man who he caught poaching from his fishponds. He refused to send him to the magistrates, much to the chagrin of his friends. I chose one of Shenstone's poems to include here:

Ye gentle Nymphs and generous Dames,
That rule o'er every British mind!
Be sure ye soothe their amorous flames,
Be sure your laws are not unkind:
For hard it is to wear their bloom

In unremitting sighs away;
To mourn the night's oppressive gloom,
And faintly bless the rising day.
And cruel 'twere a freeborn swain,
A British youth, should vainly moan;
Who, scornful of a tyrant's chain,
Submits to yours, and yours alone.
Nor pointed spear, nor links of steel,
Could e'er those gallant minds subdue,
Who Beauty's wounds with pleasure feel,
And boast the fetters wrought by you.

Dudley poet and rhymist Ben Boucher is a man of whom it was said:

Oh! Rare Ben Boucher, Boucher Ben;
The best of poets, but worst of men.

Ben wrote in one poem of the horse of a certain tailor in the town, which was not in the best of conditions:

His back is both long and thin
His belly has got no corn therein
He looks both naked and forlorn
And takes the whip instead of corn.

Ben was fond of his beer, and raised money to buy it by writing doggerel songs and selling them in the streets. Eventually he found his way to the workhouse, where he died in 1851, aged 82.

16

BLACK COUNTRY BLUE PLAQUES

Blue Plaques are used to denote places where significant people or places are or were located. There are plenty around the Black Country, especially in Wolverhampton, where the Civic Society has erected over ninety plaques in recent years. Here are just a few from around the region.

Julius Alfred Chatwin was an architect, mainly working on churches. One work was Lloyds Bank in Queen Square, Wolverhampton, where he has a plaque to commemorate his work.

In Walsall there are a number of plaques recognising poet Henry Newbolt, author Jerome K. Jerome, Dorothy Wyndlow Pattison (Sister Dora), James Thompson VC and historian, artist and photographer William 'Billy' Meikle.

In West Bromwich Madeleine Carroll, actress and humanitarian, is recognised. As is another VC hero, Robert Edwin Phillips, from Hill Top.

In Lye there is a plaque on the library wall remembering Sir Cedric Hardwicke, a famous Lye film star, born in 1893.

Dudley-born football star Duncan Edwards has a statue in Dudley, and a blue plaque in Stretford where he lived when he played for Manchester United.

Black Country comedienne Dolly Allen has a plaque at Brierley Hill Civic Hall. Another Black Country comedian, Harry Harrison, is remembered with a plaque in Tipton.

A Wolverhampton plaque remembers Gwen Berryman. Gwen played Doris Archer from the long-running radio soap. Gwen died in 1983 and her plaque is on Goldthorn Hill Road, near Blakenhall.

17

BLACK COUNTRY MEDALLISTS

VICTORIA CROSS

Walsall is the home of two holders of the Victoria Cross. The first is John Henry Carless who was born in November 1896. His childhood was spent in Caldmore and he attended St Mary's Roman Catholic School. In 1910 he played in the finals of the English Schools soccer shield and won a gold medal. He then worked as a currier in a local leather works.

In August 1914 war in Europe changed life for many young men, and patriotic fever spread across the nation; Carless was one of thousands who volunteered to fight for King and Country. He applied to join the Royal Navy and joined on 1 September 1915. Carless was willing to 'have a go'. Early in his career he helped rescue passengers from a beleaguered hospital ship and saved a stoker enveloped in flames during a boiler room fire.

On 11 November 1917, exactly one year before the Armistice was signed, Carless was called to battle stations for what was to be one of the vital sea battles of the war: Helgoland Blight. Battle commenced on 17 November and Carless's ship HMS *Caledon*, was shelled heavily. Carless was working as a rammer at a gun when a shell splinter hit him; he suffered abdominal injuries which would kill him a short while later. Crippled with pain, Carless carried on in his duties despite knowing he had received a fatal wound.

Carless assisted in moving injured men around him. He collapsed, but got up and continued his work until he finally collapsed again and died from his wounds. Six months later, Ordinary Seaman John Henry Carless received the Victoria Cross for his bravery in action. The citation read: 'For most conspicuous bravery and devotion to duty.'

John's parents received the award from King George V at Buckingham Palace. In 1920 a memorial to Carless was unveiled in front of the Public Library and in 1923 there was further recognition when Oxford Street, Caldmore, was renamed Carless Street, and Regent Street, Pleck, was renamed Caledon Street.

Another Walsall VC was Charles Bonner, who joined the Royal Navy at a young age. He served with great distinction in the First World War and in 1916 was awarded the Distinguished Service Cross. In 1917 Bonner was awarded the Victoria Cross for 'conspicuous gallantry and consummate skills and coolness in action with an enemy submarine'. He had the honour of meeting the king before any public announcement was made of the award.

Bonner was a Lieutenant on a 'Q' ship, a heavily disguised vessel that looked harmless, but was designed to lure German submarines to them and sink them. They were heavily armed, with highly trained crews. In August 1917 a desperate tussle took place between a U-boat and Bonner's ship. His ship was damaged, on fire and in danger of exploding, but still they engaged the U-boat.

Torpedoes were fired and missed and the 'Q' ship had to be abandoned. Bonner played a gallant part in the action and escaped death, but was wounded. The mystery of the 'Q' ships had been revealed. Bonner survived the war and died, age 67, in 1951.

In 1918 Lance Corporal George Onions from Bilston was awarded a VC. He was one of two soldiers who captured 200 prisoners, when he reported an enemy counter-attack. The moral is, don't mess with Bilston people.

A Victoria Cross award was made to Dudley's John Berryman. He won it through his bravery at the Charge of the Light Brigade, during the battle of Balaclava in 1854. In that action only 195 from 678 men survived. Troop Sergeant Berryman's horse was shot from under him and he joined Captain Webb, who had been badly wounded.

Berryman and two colleagues carried Webb out of range of the Russian guns. Sadly Webb died later from his wounds but all three rescuers were awarded the VC. Berryman was a professional soldier who also saw action in the Indian Mutiny in 1857 and during the Zulu Wars in 1883, when he was aged 54. He retired with the rank of major in 1883 and died in 1896, following a long illness.

GEORGE MEDAL

Black Country George Medal Winners include Evelyn Gertrude Thomas and Lisa Potts. The George Medal was instituted in September 1940, to reward and recognise acts of great bravery and was mainly intended for civilians. Only four people from the Black Country received this honour during the Second World War. Three of those were from West Bromwich and the fourth from Walsall.

Evelyn Gertrude Thomas and Doctor William Stanley Walton were a matron and doctor at the District General Hospital in West Bromwich. They were on duty during a heavy bombing raid on 19 November 1940 which started large fires in two buildings near the hospital.

Doctor Walton left the control room in the Town Hall to carry out a survey of casualty services. He assisted in putting out fires caused by incendiary devices and then noticed that the hospital laundry was on fire, as well as other nearby buildings. As Thomas and Walton discussed evacuation, a bomb fell and demolished the laundry building. This helped Walton make the difficult decision to evacuate.

Their citations stated that the two provided leadership and initiative, which was a great factor in the successful evacuation. During the evacuation, the hospital and its surroundings were under constant attack. This was the most destructive air raid on West Bromwich during the war.

Another recipient was Miss Charity Bick, an ARP despatch rider. During the aforementioned air raid, Miss Bick assisted her father, the senior post warden at the Sams Lane post. They were attempting to put out one of three incendiary bombs in a shop roof using a stirrup pump and buckets of water. During the attempt Charity fell through the roof and sustained minor injuries. She and her father returned to the ARP post.

High explosive bombs began to fall and the explosion threw them off their feet. During the bombardment Miss Bick made several journeys to the control room, a distance of 1¾ miles. Her actions released other ARP wardens for duty. Most notable was that Charity was only 14 years old at the time. She had lied when asked her age, with her father's knowledge and permission. She was the youngest person to receive the George Medal.

A Historical Society blue plaque was unveiled at the Lyng School in West Bromwich in Charity's honour a few years ago. There is a portrait of Charity on display at the Imperial War Museum, London, and Charity Bick Way, a street in West Bromwich, was also named in her honour.

The last, but not least, recipient during the Second World War, Richard Noel Hateley, was involved during heavy bombing at a gas holder at Pleck. Richard was a Superintendent at Walsall Gas Department.

He and two others put themselves in great danger by fighting the fire, which had caused the holder to sink to near the ground. There was a great risk of explosion during the rescue and Hateley was never more than 3ft from the gas holder.

A modern day George Medal recipient was nursery nurse Lisa Potts. On 8 July 1996, while involved in a teddy bears' picnic for nursery children, Lisa noticed a man run around the side of the nursery carrying a large knife and attack a number of the mothers. The man then began to attack the children and also Lisa when she tried to protect them.

Lisa sustained horrific injuries, but continued protecting the children, ushering them away. She suffered shocking injuries, requiring forty-five stitches on one hand alone, and a chipped skull. Whilst in hospital she remained more concerned for the injured children than her own health.

Lisa's heroism was praised universally. In the Queen's Birthday Honours List in 1997 she was awarded the George Medal 'For services in saving the lives of a number of children from a man armed with a machete, despite being severely injured herself'. Lisa received her award from the Queen in November 1997.

Recovery was long and hard. Lisa was unable to continue teaching; she endured absences for frequent hospital visits and had severe flashbacks and excruciating pain in one arm. She reluctantly left teaching to make a fresh start and became involved in charitable causes.

Lisa has since written a number of books, including her autobiography *Beyond the Smile*. In 2000 she began a counselling degree at Wolverhampton College, and has turned her life around with a new role in caring.

18

BLACK COUNTRY LIFE

The Black Country dialect is an almost unique feature and another facet of our region often subject to reasoned debate. Do we just have an accent, or is it a proper dialect? We certainly speak differently to our Birmingham neighbours, who have an accent. A dialect can be identified by the form of words used, not only by the way people speak.

Black Country 'spake' has been described as the nearest thing to Chaucerian English, and is also said to have Germanic influences. Sub-dialects existed depending on the trade; for example nail makers spoke a different set of words to foundry workers or chain makers.

With a massive population increase during the Industrial Revolution, you might think our dialect would have been diluted. This was not the case. Immigrants working in trades had to learn the local dialect to understand the job and to talk to the locals and so adopted our dialect.

Some Black Country words and sayings are still in use today by both older residents and the younger generations 'brought up proper'. These include:

Chunter – ceaselessly talk in a low tone.

Tranklements – knick-knacks, gee-gaws or useless pieces of bric-a-brac.

Boffombled – unable to grasp the significance, lose the thread.

Yampy – not the 'full shilling', 'short of a marble or two' (in a harmless way).

Werrit – worry

Crowsen-end – mining term from the Lower Gornal area. It describes the hole in the ground where subsidence caused part of the roof to collapse into the workings.

'Big as a bonk 'oss' – a well-proportioned woman or girl, can also apply to men and boys.

'Get yer feet in the sawdust' – spending time in the pub, often said by a disgruntled wife.

'As arf-ish as a railout' – needs an intermediate translation: 'half-ish' = 'half-soaked' = 'slow on the uptake'. So, the saying can be translated to read 'as half-soaked as a real lout'.

'Looks as though the trams 'an gone by' – would be uttered if the recipients teacup had not been filled properly.

An expression used in the Black Country is 'silly juggins' to describe someone who has committed a stupid act. Juggins was actually a person, first name Richard, born in Darlaston in 1843. He instigated the coming together of several small Black Country unions as the Midland Counties Trades Federation, and wielded considerable influence as its secretary.

It seems he had picked up the 'silly' tag when he was young. Dictionaries define a Juggins as a silly person or simpleton, a description that clearly does not describe Richard.

Black Country humour is often based around dialect. Here are some of the best examples, in my humble opinion:

A man going to his wife's funeral was asked by the undertaker to ride with his mother-in-law. He said he would do it, but added: 'Doh forget, yom agooin to spile me day.'

Also on death, a widow had her husband's ashes placed in an egg timer after his cremation. She explained, 'he day do any werk wen 'e wuz alive, I'm gooin ter mek sure he is useful now 'es jed'.

Not necessarily humour, but a tale of a Black Country workman, who always took a bottle of cold tea to work. One day he exclaimed 'I cor get me tay bottle in me pocket, me wench'. His wife retorted, 'Then pour a drop out yer fule.'

Gornal people have often been the subject of jokes. In particular the stupidity of the comedy duo Aynuck and Ayli is famed around the region:
'We're yo' gooin' this morning?'
'Ter waerk, what did yo' think?'
'But yo'm on yer way home'
'Oh arr, soo I am. I turned me back ter the wind ter light me fag an' fergot ter turn round agen'

On my travels I have come across a few 'unusual' names given to Black Country children, here are just a few:
'Anchor Wright' Brindley – (1763), buried in 1764 as 'Anchorite' Brindley
Prince Henry Earp
John Back Wenlock Ellis – (does this signify where he was conceived?)
Sobieke – possibly born to Stuart sympathisers as the Old Pretender married the Polish Princess Maria Celementina Sobieski.

Biblical names recorded in Old Swinford were: Abraham, Obadiah, Barnabas, Tobias and Cornelius. Unusual names recorded in Old Swinford were: Mehetabel ('whom God benefits'), Golibra, Caranappa, Sergeant and Theophilus (could mean 'friend of God').

The 1901 census recorded 761 dwellings in Cradley; of those 37 per cent made chains and 28 per cent made nails. None of the dwellings had running water or a bathroom and lighting in the houses was by candle or oil lamp.

There were no carpets on the quarry tile floors and rugs were 'podged' to cover them. Children left school at 13 and took up work in a factory. Many of the older women were illiterate, having been born before the passing of the Education Act 1870. Life was tough, with long hours and physical work.

Wife selling took place in a number of towns in the region in the eighteenth and nineteenth centuries. Gornal and Tipton were both the location for a number of sales. Until the end of the 1800s many men saw women as chattels. It was a harsh life for women, many being treated worse than animals. They had poor health, worked hard, were constantly pregnant and were often abused terribly by their husbands.

The selling of wives, subject to certain formalities, was seen as legal (although it wasn't). For poor people it was the only escape from a marriage; the first divorce courts were only set up in 1857, before then a special Act of Parliament was required to end a marriage.

A wife was often not consulted on their sale until the day. Sales were for many reasons, such as nagging, being infertile and being too head-strong. At the sale a halter was often placed over the wife's neck, a rope attached and the woman led to the marketplace. A crier was hired to attract bidders.

On occasions there was a private arrangement between the husband and the buyer, though the auction still had to take place for it to be 'legal'. Sales realised between 6*d* and half-a-crown and were often a spectacle for locals to enjoy. Some were amicable and not all husbands were cruel. Second marriages were, however, bigamous and often led to court proceedings.

One example was that of a 20-year-old wife, a poor slip of a girl who appeared half-starved. Bidding ended at 6*d* (2½ pence) and her new husband vowed to 'put some flesh on 'er bones'. He was good to his promise and she bore him a number of children, three of whom later became school teachers.

19

RUNNING THE BLACK COUNTRY

In 1295 Dudley was represented in Parliament by Benedict, son of Andrew, and a lawyer called Randolph. These were the last representatives until 1832, when Sir John Campbell took up the position of Member of Parliament.

The reason for the gap was simple; the good people of Dudley refused to pay the expenses for a Member of Parliament because they felt it was an unnecessary cost. In 1832 the Reform Act changed the electoral system of England and Wales and the MP was no longer a cost to the constituents.

Charles S. Forster, Member of Parliament for Walsall from 1832 to 1841, famously said in a speech that he wished the world's dust might be swept by Walsall brushes.

In 1885 Sir Benjamin Hingley was elected as Liberal MP for North Worcestershire. Hingley was son of chain maker Noah Hingley and lived at Hatherton Lodge, Drews Holloway in Halesowen.

In the 1908 General Election, Lois Dawson was the only woman to vote. She claimed she was the Louis Dawson on the electoral register for Wolverhampton East and voted successfully. The first time women were allowed to vote was in 1918 in the December General Election. This was brought about by the passing of the Qualification of Women Act.

Dudley's Labour MP George Wigg was the man who exposed John Profumo, then Secretary of State for War. Profumo had an infamous affair with Christine Keeler in 1963 and Wigg used Parliamentary procedure to expose it. George left Parliament in 1967 with a life peerage as Baron Wigg of the Borough of Dudley.

The first woman to breastfeed at Westminster was Wolverhampton-born Helene Valerie Hayman. As Baroness Hayman she was the first Lord Speaker of the House of Lords, owing to constitutional reform which saw the Lord Chancellor role being separated from that of Speaker. She attended Wolverhampton Girls' High School. When she first entered Parliament in 1974, aged 25, she became the youngest member of the House of Commons, remaining the 'baby of the house' until 1977.

Walsall Mayors date back to 1377. The first recorded mayor was Nicholas Flaxhall in 1452.

The Walsall Coat of Arms features the bear and ragged staff associated with Warwickshire. This is due to Walsall being passed to the Earls of Warwick in 1390, who were lords of the manor until 1488.

In Dudley, the first mayor was Humphrey Jukes in 1584.

The first Wolverhampton Mayor, in 1848, was the ironmaster George Benjamin Thorneycroft (1791–1851). He owned the Shrubbery Ironworks in Horseley Fields, Wolverhampton. His statue stands in the old Town Hall in Wolverhampton.

In 1882 Reuben Farley was the only candidate suggested for the new mayoral position in West Bromwich. He became mayor five times in the town.

The first mayor of Bilston Borough was Herbert Beach who served from September 1933 to 1935.

The first in Tipton was Arthur Frederick Welch, who served from 1938.

During the nineteenth century, local authorities emerged and took on the role of organising and providing services for their residents. There were County Councils, but another layer of administration was the Urban District Council (UDC).

Brierley Hill UDC was created in 1894 and responsible for delivering services within a small area in South Staffordshire. In the vicinity were Quarry Bank and Kingswinford District Councils, showing just how local they were. By 1934 smaller councils were merging to create larger local councils, which were also merged in 1966 when they all joined with Dudley.

In 1974 the Black Country was divided into four authorities: Sandwell, Walsall, Wolverhampton and Dudley, which covered the Black Country within a wider West Midlands. At first this confused people, where did they belong: Halesowen, West Midlands, Black Country or ...?

Now local communities refer to themselves by whichever town or village they live, the authority comes next and the 'West Midlands' often seems to be an add-on, saved for addressing envelopes!

Cradley had its own 'Little Parliament' with events sometimes similar to those in the House of Commons. The first public meeting, to discuss the creation of Cradley Parish Council, took place in 1894.

One speaker, Mr Homer, suggested that whoever was chosen should be the most intellectual and from the people who pay most tax. This was not well received, it was pointed out that there are plenty of great taxpayers who have no brains!

An election took place a month later and the meeting room was packed. Thirty-one candidates stood for fifteen councillors and each voter had fifteen votes. It seems the process worked, with candidates being drawn from across Cradley Society, not just one class. However, Cradley Parish Council was short-lived and ended in March 1925.

Stan Hill became the youngest civic head in the country at 26, when he became chair of Brierley Hill UDC. In this role he attended a Royal Reception in Stafford and was asked by

Prince Philip what the council's motto: '*Sine Labore Nihil Floret*' meant in English. Of course, it means: 'Without labour nothing flourishes' knowledge duly imparted to the Prince.

Early attempts to provide fire fighting services came in the 1830s. In Dudley the borough bought its own engines in the 1870s and they were manned by police constables. The police stations at Dudley, Netherton, Woodside and Kates Hill all served as fire stations.

A voluntary fire brigade existed in Stourbridge as early as 1904. It responded to a fire at Enville Hall. They had a horse-drawn engine and had been alerted by a young man who had cycled from the scene. The engine had a steam pump which pumped 300 gallons a minute, said to be the first engine of its type in a provincial town in England.

The police also ran ambulance and fire services in Wolverhampton. Between the wars twenty-four constables were paid an extra 2*s* a week to be firemen and the police also manned the ambulance.

20

THE BLACK COUNTRY OVERSEAS

There are a number of towns with the name Dudley. In the USA there is a Dudley in Massachusetts, Missouri, Georgia, North Carolina and Pennsylvania. I have only visited one – the Georgia outpost. It has two churches and a diner but not a lot else. In the 2000 census it had 447 residents and was founded in 1902.

There is also a Dudley South in Gippsland, Victoria, Australia. Built to service a section of the state coal mine in the area, it is now part of the State Coal Mine Heritage area.

Tipton is another Black Country town with 'branches' overseas. There are Tipton Counties in the USA in Tennessee and Indiana, and towns in Iowa, Missouri and California. The California Tipton is located just north of Los Angeles.

It appears that Cradley has no international namesakes, but Cradley in Herefordshire is the largest village in that county and Cradley parish is also the largest in Herefordshire.

Miners from the Black Country immigrated to Vancouver Island because coal was discovered in the 1830s. The Hudson's Bay Company set up a base there, intending to use the coal to fuel their ship *Beaver* as well as supplying naval vessels. A settlement, Nanaimo, was built and families moved in.

Unfortunately there was an acute shortage of miners and it was decided to recruit some. The Black Country was the area chosen for that recruitment campaign. Conditions in the Black Country were poor: health, wages, housing and food were all below standard.

The first recruit was George Robinson, who signed on as manager of the company's Coal and Brick Works. He then recruited twenty colliers, many of them with families and so a total of eighty-three made the journey.

Workers came from Buckpool, Bromley, Commonside, Dudley and other local towns. The party began their journey to a new life on the *Princess Royal*. The journey was terrible, with two adults and four children dying on the voyage.

The workers made a success of their emigration. In the 1950s the British Columbia Historical Society wrote to Brierley Hill council stating they were preparing to mark the centenary of the journey with a re-enactment, and the vice-president of the Society visited Brierley Hill.

21

BLACK COUNTRY MARKETS AND SHOPPING

In 1824 Walsall had one of the largest pig markets in the country. It was in prime position off the High Street and reflected a professional side of a great Black Country tradition, whereby working men kept a pig in the back garden to be slaughtered to provide meat for the family.

This practice did not die out until after the Second World War and it does remind me of another Black Country joke:
'Is yer fairther in?'

'No 'es in the pig sty, yo cor miss 'im, 'es the one wi' t'hat on.'

In the late nineteenth century, local authorities began a campaign to stop this practice of keeping pigs. Sanitary conditions were top priorities to reduce incidences of cholera and the like among the over-crowded communities in rapidly growing Black Country towns.

Firkins is a name well known throughout the Black Country. Their beginnings are back in the 1870s when Mary Firkin started a pork pie shop in Carters Green, West Bromwich. By the First World War the company was winning medals for its pies.

Expansion in the 1960s saw the company take over Robinson's shops, and Reynolds and Hughes in Dudley. Sadly in 2011 the company bakery in Black Lake, West Bromwich closed due to the recession, though the thirty-three shops were saved.

Teddy Gray's is a sweet shop institution, based in Dudley. It was first founded by John Gray in 1826, who bought and sold sweets. John's son Teddy was the one who made the business what it is today. Another Teddy Gray perfected the famous herbal tablet in the 1920s. This is the sweet that most people associate with the company.

After the Second World War, the company began opening more shops as far afield at Bewdley. To date, five generations of the Gray family have run the business, with three generations working together today. Herbals are sold widely; they have been imitated but never bettered.

The Co-operative movement established societies around the Black Country. By the mid-1980s, however, the Co-op was disappearing from our High Streets. The movement started in Rochdale in 1844, but there were Co-ops in the Black Country in the late 1700s, for example in Wolverhampton.

There was plenty of Co-op activity in the 1860s, with small societies in Lye, West Bromwich and West Smethwick. By the twentieth century, Co-op activity was professionalising, with central premises, warehouses, baking and milk delivery.

A Co-op existed in Walsall in 1862 and had 166 members, but it struggled for five years. A further society in the town came and went in 1874, but in 1886 the third Co-op stayed the course and celebrated fifty years in business in 1936. It absorbed the Wolverhampton and District society in 1972.

The Co-op was more than a shop. They provided education and became part of the community, also diversifying into many areas of local life, such as insurance and funerals. Elements of the businesses still survive today.

Some say Merry Hill has ruined town centre shopping, but others extoll the virtues of the employment and variety of shopping that is on offer under one roof. It has transformed the industrial wasteland that followed the closure of Round Oak.

Early building was not on the brownfield, but nearby on greenfield land. This did provoke opposition, but later as the sprawling site grew it took in the Level Street part of the landscape and much more beside.

1982 – Merry Hill Farm was purchased by the Richardson Brothers, Don and Roy.

1984 – construction began on the first phase.

1985 – first three stores opened, including MFI.

1986 – second phase, including Carrefour hypermarket opened. It lasted two years, then Gateway took over and finally ASDA, who are there today.

1987 – further expansion took place.

1988 – early in the year, upper level shops opened. Later the ten-screen cinema complex opened.

1989 – Jules Verne food court opened, the one with the big balloon in the middle. It only lasted two years before it closed.

1989 – construction began on the Waterfront. It ran to three phases of offices, restaurants and bars and was completed in 1995.

1990 – the final phase was completed, Sainsbury's and Marks & Spencer being two major names who moved in.

Not everything went smoothly. You may remember the monorail, an expensive train set, designed to link the old

Round Oak railway station with the Waterfront, Merry Hill bus station and the boulevard stores. It closed due to safety concerns and a fall-out between the owners of Merry Hill and the Waterfront. It was also planned for the monorail to join the Midland Metro tram, but this never materialised.

Future development has been mooted. John Lewis and House of Fraser may be coming to Merry Hill and there is talk of greater integration with Brierley Hill town centre, but at the time of writing these are on hold because of the current (2013) financial position.

At the time of writing, Merry Hill has over 80,000 'likes' on Facebook, and nearly 140,000 admit on Facebook to having been there.

Dudley number 1 canal passes through the waterfront.

There have been four owners of Merry Hill: the Richardsons, Mountleigh, Chelsfield and current owners Westfield.

There are over 250 stores in the complex.

Merry Hill has (in part) led to the disappearance of 'big name' stores nearby, especially in Dudley.

Free parking at Merry Hill seems to have been part of this, especially when Dudley MBC announced car park charges; how long though before Merry Hill begins charging?

The onsite cinema was the first multiplex built in Dudley borough, and the first new cinema in Dudley for fifty years.

FOOD AND DRINK

Black Country Bostin' Fittle has been served for generations. It is not haute cuisine, but has largely stood the test of time. The phrase inspired *Bostin' Fittle*, the recipe book, as well as a pub located just up the road from the Black Country Living Museum.

In 1909 the Dowager Countess of Dudley, Georgina, published her *Dudley Book of Cooking and Household Recipes*. She followed this with a second book of Christmas recipes. They included one for mincemeat to fill mince pies, involving 2lb of beef fillet and 1lb of beef suet among its ingredients.

Eating habits of the Black Country were simple:

Sunday – hot meat day
Monday – cold meat day
Tuesday – hash day
Wednesday – cabbage and bacon day
Thursday – bread and cheese day
Friday – clam day (clammed or clemmed = hungry)
Saturday – drunk all day

Did Grorty Pudding evolve in the Black Country? Some say yes, but by accident, to feed large families in the nineteenth century. It was a cheap, filling dish and easy to prepare; yes it took ages to cook, but needed little attention.

I have fond memories of eating grorty pudding on bonfire night in the 1960s around a huge bonfire, with lots of fireworks and plenty of food. Those days are long gone, but to my mind grorty pudding was always the tastiest food eaten that night.

One theory of the Grorty Pudding origin is that the recipe is very old, as far back as the eleventh century. It involved a Norman chieftain and his personal chef, one Richard de Grote. Richard fell in love with a young kitchen maid from Cradley.

It is said he created a dish as a joke for his love, to suit her more simple tastes. She apparently christened it 'Grorty Dick' after her lover. I think I prefer the more plausible nineteenth-century origin of the dish, but wouldn't it be nice to declare it was 800 years older?

The recipe is 1lb shin or neck of beef, 1/2lb white groats and a sliced medium-sized onion. Place the meat and onion in a casserole; wash the groats and add those, then cover with water. Simmer on a low heat for 6 hours or longer, stirring occasionally.

The meat will be shredded,
so mix well with the
other ingredients. Give it
more flavour by adding
in some fried bacon.

A local Walsall recipe,
recorded in an 1883
collection, was for a
restorative soup:
1lb neck or knuckle of veal
1lb neck or knuckle
of mutton
1lb shin of beef
3½ pints of water
Cut the meat into small
pieces and strip from the
bone. Remove the fat, but
keep the skin. Place them all

into a saucepan and add water and salt. Cover the pan, bring
to the boil, and simmer slowly for 4 to 5 hours. Strain into a
basin, cool and remove any fat.

Well known fizzy pop Tizer first appeared in 1924 and was
originally made in a factory on Friar Park Road, Wednesbury.
The factory site is now part of a housing estate and the Tizer
brand was acquired by A.G. Barr in 1972 for £2.5 million.

In the Staffordshire part of the Black Country, elderberry
wine was made from the ripe fruit and drunk as mulled wine
at Christmas.

Pork scratchings are a Black Country delicacy. They started
out by being made from scraps of meat left once pork fat had
been rendered down. These softer scratchings were often called
'leaf'; these can still be bought, but are a rarity these days.
    The crunchy pub snacks we know and love may only
have originated in the 1970s, but have largely taken over the
market, along with the 'puffy' pork crunch. Their fame has

spread across the country, with bags of the salty and tasty snack hanging from many a pub wall. Pork crunch is also made in other parts of the world, often flavoured with chilli, garlic and the like.

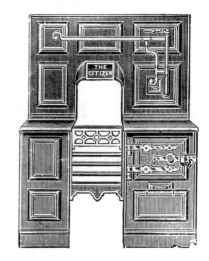

Black pudding is something else made as part of the need to use the whole of the pig. It was made from the blood, with added oatmeal and fat. It is not an exclusive Black Country product however, 'blood sausage' is made around the world with many local variants.

The Black Country variety has vied for years with Bury black pudding from Lancashire. It is a versatile food and can be eaten cooked for breakfast, or raw, especially accompanying a cheese and onion sandwich. Ma Pardoe's used to serve 'black pudding thermidor' as a starter; far more tasty than lobster!

Modern black pudding often has much of the fat removed and therefore loses some of its flavour, but authentic versions can still be found, thank goodness.

22

LEISURE, ENTERTAINMENT AND CELEBRATION

THEATRE AND CINEMA

The theatre and cinema has always had a strong presence in the Black Country. Before the advent of television, Variety Theatre was popular entertainment, possibly because it was combined with another local pastime: drinking ale!

In Smethwick a Christmas tradition was for the mummers to present a Christmas Play. F.W. Hackwood described their activities: '... dressed fantastically in paper and tinsel, and coloured rags: some with blacked and some with floured faces; some wearing masks, some with fake beards and wigs'.

The Grand Theatre at Wolverhampton opened in 1894. It became the home for a repertory company for twenty-five years and hosted many famous personalities, such as leading Shakespearean actress Ellen Terry, Charlie Chaplin and Norman Wisdom. The Grand did have hard times and closed for a time in the 1970s, but it is now a thriving theatre again.

Oscar Deutsch and the Odeon had a strong connection to the Black Country. Birmingham-born Deutsch was influential in the cinema world in the 1920s and 1930s. He was the man behind the Odeon cinema chain.

His Black Country connection was that he built his first cinema in 1928 in Brierley Hill. Although he opened his first cinema in 1920, this was the first he had built. Initially known as 'The Picture House', it was renamed The Odeon in 1936. Deutsch employed a Stourbridge architect, Stanley Griffiths, to design it.

Odeon Theatres at first concentrated on Birmingham and West Midlands locations, but eventually spread country-wide. The art deco Odeon style set them apart from other picture houses, with Deutsch using bold distinctive colours in addition to glass features.

It was an occasion to visit an Odeon, the name 'Odeon', according to the Odeon Company, stood for 'Oscar Deutsch Entertains Our Nation'. After Deutsch died of cancer in 1941, the chain was sold to J. Arthur Rank.

Dudley Hippodrome is famous for two events. It is said to have been the first provincial theatre to present Bob Hope and Laurel and Hardy. The first televised pantomime was also staged there in 1951.

It has been closed since 2009 and (in 2013) it is under threat of demolition. The group that has been formed to save the theatre say that in the twenty-first century it is an important building and should be preserved and be returned to its former glory.

CELEBRATIONS AND FESTIVALS

Mothering Sunday in the Black Country was a day to be celebrated. It used to be in the calendar on the fourth Sunday of Lent. Today, thanks to American GIs in England during the Second World War, it has moved to the second Sunday in March.

The traditional meal for many was roast veal and custard (we had veal with milk gravy when I was a young boy). Another popular Black Country dish served on Mothering Sunday was frumenty, made from the gleanings of corn. The grain was soaked in water for hours and then put into the pot. It was stewed until soft and served with milk together with sugar or treacle.

May Day had its own customs in the Black Country. In the nineteenth century they would go out into the country to imbibe a whey drink. This was made with rum (surprise, surprise!) and milk. Once drunk, our ancestors ran races, fought pitched battles and generally left a trail of havoc and destruction behind them. Sound familiar?

The successful conclusion of conflict is often celebrated. The Napoleonic Wars had profound impact on Great Britain, and the Black Country played its role in supplying equipment such as gun locks. Many local men joined the army and fought in campaigns.

In 1813 Stourbridge held a series of celebrations when it was thought Napoleon Bonaparte had finally been vanquished. There were 'great demonstrations of joy' after the memorable allied victory at Leipzig; however this was somewhat premature.

In June 1814, the second Revolutionary War ended when Napoleon was 'safely' banished to Elba on Corsica and there were further festivities. In Stourbridge an ox was roasted and sheep were dressed and given to the poor. There was a great procession along High Street, with trumpeters on horseback and the Royal Standard flying

There was also a band, six constables, four magistrates and seven professional gentlemen. '10 sheep placed one on the other to form a triangle' and a 'very fine baron of beef decorated with ribbons' were also part of the procession. Spectators lined the route to the Grammar School, where 'God Save the King' and 'Rule Britannia' were sung. The following day the sheep were roasted around the town; 4,000 children received a piece of plum pudding and the beef of two oxen were consumed.

However, Napoleon escaped from his exile, raised an army and embarked on his hundred-day campaign, which culminated in his final defeat at Waterloo in 1815. Celebrations to mark this event were much more subdued.

The Coronation of King George IV took place in July 1820. A subscription was raised in Dudley to pay for a dinner for the poor, and to regale the children of the Sunday Schools and Schools of Industry in the parish. There were parades in the streets; four sheep were roasted in the Market Place and served with a large quantity of ale.

All the shops, except the pubs, closed for the day. The main street was utterly crowded from end to end. Town gents and Dudley yeomanry met at the Assembly Room and, in the late evening, the yeomanry became unruly and began to fight amongst themselves.

The fight became a 'battle royal', with furniture, bottles and glasses being thrown. Missiles rained down on the crowds outside and they retaliated, throwing missiles back up. Two or three dozen windows were broken. To distract the mob, the gaslights in the town were lit and the planned firework display started, which did the trick. The yeomanry were blamed for starting what could have degenerated into a full-scale riot.

The 1951 Festival of Britain was not only a London event. Dudley held its own, called the 'Pageant of Dudley'. There were six organising committees and a stage was built in the castle courtyard seating 2,500. The pageant ran for ten nights.

It had been sponsored by the Council, but organised by townspeople. There were nine episodes and a finale; subjects included the death of Harold at Hastings, the visit to Dudley of Queen Elizabeth in 1575 and the part played by the castle in the English Civil War, with the finale focusing on Dudley in 1951. Sadly, bad weather meant attendances were low and a loss of £3,000 was the result.

LEISURE TIME

In 1911 Dudley saw the first Members of Parliament to fly above the Black Country. This took place at Dudley Castle fetes, held in the Castle grounds. In 1911 John Norton-Griffiths, Conservative MP for Wednesbury, experienced 'a graceful ascent' from the castle courtyard. The balloon eventually came down safely near Coventry Road outside Birmingham.

Next day Conservative Dudley MP, Lieutenant-Colonel Arthur Sackville Trevor Griffiths-Boscowen had a similar experience.

Mrs Griffiths-Boscowen expressed a wish to accompany Arthur, but the balloonist in charge felt her additional weight might overload the carrier and she was left behind. The balloon made a safe landing at Bridgnorth.

Griffiths-Boscowen was knighted a few days later, probably nothing to do with his adventure.

Dudley Castle fetes ended just after the First World War, but the grounds remained open to the public. In 1937 Dudley Zoo opened on a 40 acre site; uniquely animals were not caged, but kept in enclosures. There were several disused surface mineral workings in the grounds which were put to innovative use as open-air pits for animals.

The zoo and castle contain twelve listed buildings including the castle, as well as the turnstile entrance which is an early example of concrete architecture. In its time, the zoo was home to elephants, which are now no longer present, and 'Cuddles' the famous killer whale.

There are currently over 1,000 animals in the zoo. There is a chairlift, refurbished in 2012 and there are development plans to join the zoo to the Black Country Living Museum and Dudley Canal Trust; it is planned for all three attractions to share a single entrance from 2014.

Before Dudley Zoo there were travelling shows bringing wild animals to audiences. One troupe that visited the Black Country was Wombwell's Wild Beasts. But things did not always go according to plan, after all these were wild beasts. In West Bromwich in 1857 a tiger and a lion fought each other to death. The beasts had adjoining cages and the tiger escaped and attacked the lion.

All the keepers could do was watch the fight, which was heard all over the town, as the tiger killed the lion. An extra-strong cage, made of sheet iron, was made for the tiger, as it instantly became a major attraction.

Pigeon flying may have been the only pastime of many Black Country colliers. It does still have its devotees, but not as many as in the late nineteenth and early twentieth centuries.

Our pigeon flyers used to back their own birds in races and much money changed hands.

One old collier on his death bed was visited by the vicar. The collier asked about what came after death: 'Shall we have wings, parson?' The response was yes angels did have wings. The collier replied: 'Well ... if yo' has wings and I 'as wings, when yo' come up I'll fly yer for a 'quid".

GAMES AND PASTIMES

There were lots of old games played in the Black Country; some still being played today. Here is a small selection that Black Country folk remember from their childhood.

Duck on the Hob was played with a round pebble about 2lb in weight. Players decide (possibly by the toss of a coin) who goes first. The first player throws the 'duck' as far as possible. The other players then try to hit the 'duck' with another stone. The role is then reversed

Bunt the Ring was a local game for adults, played in Cradley Heath by chainmakers. The game was played with iron marbles, ranging in size from ping pong to tennis ball size. The rules were similar to the game of marbles we all played as children, but much harder, given the size of the 'marbles'.

Child's counting rhymes are many and varied. This one was used in Walsall for skipping:

> Racing car number nine
> Using petrol all the time
> How many gallons does it use?
> One, two, three, four ...

PUBS, INNS AND TAVERNS

The Whittington Inn, Kinver, built in 1310, is a favourite drinking spot for many. It was also reputedly the home of Dick Whittington's family. The Whittington family originated in Kinver, though Dick was born in the Forest of Dean. I could find no evidence that Dick actually lived there at any time.

Lady Jane Grey is said to have spent part of her childhood at the Whittington. She is rumoured to haunt the inn but, again, there are no records to confirm this.

In the late 1990s owners of the Wolverhampton and Dudley Breweries re-furbished the pub. They used traditional wattle and daub to retain the authenticity. The work won a Conservation and Design award from South Staffordshire District Council. The pub is now owned by Marston's Brewery.

We have a number of pub names which are unique across the country. This should help to make sure you don't go to the wrong pub!

The Blackcountryman Inn was located in Lower Church Lane in Tipton. It changed its name many years ago to reflect its clientele. It has now been demolished and houses built on the site.

The Chainmakers, at Colley Gate, was originally The Talbot up until a few years ago. Another example is Mad O'Rourkes Pie Factory in Tipton, and another Tipton favourite is The Barge and Barrel. I also doubt if there is another pub named Bostin' Fittle.

The Widders in Cradley became such after its nickname 'The Widow', a local nickname for what was The Crown in Barrack Lane.

The Crooked House, aka the 'Glynne Arms' and 'Siden House', was originally a farmhouse, condemned because of subsidence due to mining activity. The building was rescued by

Banks' Brewery and refurbished as a pub. It is one of the best-known Black Country pubs, and is where a coin placed on the bar will famously appear to roll up hill.

The Welsh Go-By is an unusual pub name and existed until the 1970s on Salop Street, Dudley. This must have been linked to the wool trade in Wolverhampton; by the fourteenth century the town was an important wool collecting centre for over 200 years. Maybe the pub was on a well-trodden route for the wool trade, or did the Welsh farmers drive their sheep all the way to Dudley Market?

PUB NICKNAMES AND ALTER-EGOS

I know of a number of pubs that have been better known by their nickname. My own knowledge is of pubs around the Dudley area, here are the ones I found:

The 'Napper' is the Saracen's Head in Dudley town centre

The British Lion in Oldbury was known as 'Pop Hadley's'

The 'Cow Shed' is the Shrewsbury Arms, in Wolverhampton Street, Dudley. It is possibly named so because 'ladies of the night' gathered here.

The Spade Makers Arms in Hunts Street was known by locals as the 'Bug and Blanket'

The 'Tatters' is the Earl of Dudley Arms on Wellington Road; it is next door to a scrapyard.

The Duck in Smethwick was known as the 'Dirty Duck' as it had a Muscovy duck on its sign.

'Ma Pardoes' is, of course, The Old White Swan in Netherton, which has the famous tin painted ceiling with pride of place being the white swan in the middle of that lovely ceiling.

'Billy Picks' is the Lyttleton Arms in Halesowen town centre, named after a previous landlord, William James Pick, licensee from 1905 to 1942.

Finally, the Golden Cross in Smethwick was known as the 'Stuffed Donkey' because there was such a beast in the passageway! Why?

BLACK COUNTRY BREWERIES

The Black Country undoubtedly brews the best mild in the world, as well as many other fine brews to boot. Documented brewing goes back to 1468 when Halesowen first licensed 'common brewers'.

During the nineteenth century, much of the beer brewed was done in licensed beer houses, where the £2 cost of the licence could quickly be recuperated. Many 'home brewers' kept on a day job, as this was a new business area and licensees were cautious to begin with.

Many previously famous brewing names have now gone, amalgamated into much larger concerns. Holden's, Batham's, Ma Pardoes, Banks's and Sarah Hughes are a few survivors.

THE GREAT OUTDOORS

The Saltwells area in Netherton is well known as a nature reserve. It was first mentioned by Doctor Plot in 1636 that there were brine springs at the site. This natural spring was not exploited until much later when the Ladywood Saline Spa opened. In 1841 it was described as: 'but a poor concern at present' and remained in existence until about 1906.

The first registered nature reserve in the United Kingdom was the Wren's Nest in 1956. The reserve is made up of Much Wenlock limestone. There over 650 types of fossil have been found, 186 fossils species were first discovered and 86 species are unique to the Wren's Nest.

In the days before package holidays, cruises and other breaks, Black Country folk had limited opportunities to get away from the grime, dirt and smog in which they lived. In 1908 nearly 2,000 hop pickers from Halesowen, Cradley Heath, Rowley and Blackheath all went by train to go hop picking in Worcestershire and Herefordshire.

By the 1930s schoolchildren had their annual summer holiday break in September; 'Gooen hoppen' was probably their main means of escape. Long trains would transport families and their luggage, including cooking utensils, to parts of Worcestershire and Herefordshire.

Pickers lived in barns, stables and pig sties, basically anywhere they could be fitted in. Food and supplies had to be delivered by van, often from their home town in the Black Country. After all, if everyone else had gone away then the shop keepers had reduced business.

There are no hop picking holidays today; machines carry out the job of the Black Country army of workers. Family holidays have replaced this most basic of breaks from routine and it won't be long before real memories of hop picking will have faded and are lost.

23

EDUCATION

BLACK COUNTRY SCHOOLS

Until the 1870 Education Act, which made basic education compulsory for all children from 5 to 13, the setting up of schools was somewhat hazard. There are some very well-established schools around the area:

1430 – The Chantry School of Holy Trinity, Stourbridge, it became King Edward VI in 1552

1512/13 – Wolverhampton Grammar School, founded by Sir Stephen Jenyns

1554 – Queen Mary's Grammar School, Walsall, founded by 'Bloody Mary'

1562 – Dudley Grammar School, it closed in 1975

1652 – Halesowen Grammar School (the Earl's)

1667 – Old Swinford Hospital School

For a small settlement, Amblecote stood out because of the number and quality of its early schools. The first was the Madras School, built in 1815, at Holloway End. It was named for the type of education system it used.

In 1846 a National School for girls and infants was opened at the junction of King William Street and Hill Street. A larger National School opened in 1857 in Coalbournbrook. National Schools provided basic education for children of poorer people.

The Amblecote Training School arrived in 1853 on the corner of High Street and Vicarage Road. It only lasted fifteen years, but in its day was an active school and well-promoted in the local community. There were also a couple of private schools, and of course Sunday School teachers were also on hand.

In the 1860s Pelsall education was provided in a room at Pelsall Ironworks, which had daily papers and periodicals for all to use. By 1868 premises were obtained for this to be extended to the whole village, probably via the Wesleyan Church and the owner of the ironworks Boaz Bloomer.

Education changed in 1870. For the first time it was obligatory for 5- to 13-year-olds to attend school. Pelsall Church School was one example. Some children were taught free of charge, through a trust, but the remainder were charged 2*d* a week.

One notable character at what was Pelsall National School was Miss Wildig. She started at the school as a pupil in 1884 and at 13 became a helper or monitor in an infants' class, earning 10s a quarter. She then became a supplementary and worked at the school until retirement in 1945. Class sizes were very large; Miss Wildig once supervised a class of 100 for a sewing lesson.

Marion Richardson was not born in the Black Country, nor did she settle here for long. However, her impact on education through both art and handwriting was enormous. Marion spent her most important teaching years, from qualification in 1912, at Dudley Girls' High School (DGHS) and at the end of her career she retired to the town.

Whilst at DGHS she organised lunch and after-school clubs, and encouraged pupils to paint and draw. The school was festooned with artwork. Marion met artist Roger Fry, famous for promoting artists such as Cezanne and Matisse. He was captivated by her pupils' art and asked for more for his London studio.

Through Roger, the Lancashire cotton trade used some of the children's block print patterns, which featured on cotton dresses sold nationwide in stores. Marion also designed workbooks and a teacher's manual for the teaching of handwriting. This helped teachers to pass on a more standardised form of handwriting and were used worldwide in primary and secondary schools. They are still widely used in a number of countries today.

24

BLACK COUNTRY TRANSPORT

FROM THE STAGECOACH TO THE MIDLAND METRO

The heyday for stage coaches was between 1780 and 1830; they lasted until better forms of transport succeeded them. Wolverhampton was the centre for Black Country coach services, some of their services were 'Beehive', 'Reindeer' and 'Emerald'. Walsall was also a regular stopping-off point.

Many coaches were named, for example 'Commodius Birmingham Diligence', which ran from Manchester through Wolverhampton and Wednesbury to Birmingham. Accidents were frequent; one in 1829 was at Monmore Green when the 'Greyhound', en route for Birmingham, broke an axle and overturned, killing one and seriously injuring four others.

Dudley was another popular coaching centre, with three termini: The Dudley Arms, The Old Bush and The Swan being their coaching inns. There are no records of coaches after 1855 when canal and railway became king.

Early roads were called turnpikes. The Black Country road system was particularly poor in the early days, partly because no Roman roads came into the region. As industry began to develop, Turnpike Trusts were set up to build new roads, but they were inadequate.

The transport of glass from Stourbridge to the river Severn was problematic because of the poor road. So much was broken en route that it could have affected the long-term development of the industry.

CANALS

Thomas Monk was a canal transport pioneer; he owned the first boatyard in Tipton. Thomas began by building boats, but moved into canal carrying. Towards the end of his career he operated a canal passenger service between Birmingham and Wolverhampton.

Long-distance canal narrow boats, even 100 years after Monk's death, were still called 'Monkey Boats' after Thomas, especially around London. Monk had a large family, some would say dynasty, of eight sons and one daughter.

All of Monk's children were trained to build boats, and they worked in boatyards throughout the Midlands, as far afield as Birmingham, Tardebigge, Warwick and Stratford. His daughter married a boat builder from Berkhamsted.

Dudley Tunnel linked limestone workings at Castle Mill with blast furnaces to the west of Dudley. It is very narrow and boatmen had to 'leg' boats through the tunnel as there was no towpath. Building the tunnel took forty years, incorporating Lord Ward's Tunnel, part of Lord Ward's Canal and the oldest of the Dudley system.

Around a dozen shafts were dug during construction, and three were retained on completion as air shafts. Only one, at Wellington Road, Queen's Cross survived. The last section completed was the Wren's Nest Tunnel and when it was finished the system comprised nearly 3 miles of tunnel around Dudley.

In 1853 over 41,000 boats passed through the system. By the 1940s traffic had dwindled and it was only used by a handful of firms. Traffic finally ceased in 1950 and the tunnel was sealed in 1962. In 1970 a large volunteer working party began restoring the tunnel.

When Dudley Council were looking for a site for a Black Country Museum, they chose an area containing the derelict Lord Ward's canal, at the start of the tunnel, which needed restoring. The rest is history and the canal and tunnel are major features of the Museum. The tunnel now forms part of the Dudley Canal Trust, which runs daily trips through the tunnel.

RAILWAYS

Railway companies began building a presence in the Black Country around the time of canal development in the early 1800s. There was a race to connect the region to other rail networks extending across the country.

In 1837 the Grand Junction Railway completed a line between Warrington and Wolverhampton and on to Birmingham. There was now a route from the docks at Liverpool, through the midlands, to London. The railway boom in the Black Country had begun.

In May 1837 the first railway line to pass near Walsall opened. The nearest station to the town was Bescot Bridge, built in 1847, with a coach service that then took passengers into Walsall town. This was the case for ten years, until a station was built in Walsall at Bridgman Place.

Other companies included the LNWR and the Oxford, Worcester and Wolverhampton Railway. In 1948, nationalisation arrived and British Railways was born. Rationalisation across the network, accelerated by Beeching in 1963, reduced drastically the mileage of track, and closed stations.

Projects such as the Midland Metro light rail, and the newly proposed High Speed railways, may shift the balance back to rail as a mode of transport.

On 20 December 1852, the Oxford, Worcester and Wolverhampton Railway opened from Wolverhampton to Evesham via Dudley. A public dinner took place to celebrate the occasion. The railway became known as the 'Old worse and worse', or 'The old wuss and wuss'.

One of the shortest regular rail journeys in the Black Country was the 5 minute trip from Dudley to Dudley Port on the train known as the 'Dudley Dasher'. It ran for 17 hours a day, averaging twenty-five trips daily, meeting every express and most local trains as they arrived at Dudley Port.

In between journeys it was used to convey Palethorpes sausage vans for transport to Dudley. The train was a way of life for factory workers travelling from Walsall into the Black Country industrial area.

Tipton once had seven passenger railway stations and six goods depots, more than many cities. This was because of the number of competing rail companies and Tipton's geographical position within the Black Country. These stations were later rationalised (another word for closed!) Prior to the railway boom Tipton had so many canals it was known as the 'Venice of the midlands'.

ON TWO WHEELS

Some of the first nationally acclaimed bicycles in the country were made by Wolverhampton's Daniel Rudge. By the end of the 1860s the velocipede had arrived from France and demand for bicycles grew rapidly.

By 1890 there were fifty-nine bicycle makers in Wolverhampton, compared with only nine for the rest of the Black Country. Firms such as Sunbeam made bicycles, before turning their attention towards making motor cars.

The best cycles were made by Major Nichols, according to many cyclists during the heyday of cycling after the Second World War. West Bromwich-born Nichols was a true Black Country man, whose father was also a cycle maker.

After school Major trained in electrical installation and worked on heavy duty projects. He joined the Navy and specialised as a Gyroscopic Compass Technician. He set up the radar control for the ship which captured the German U-boat containing the German Enigma machine and code book captured during the war.

Major developed his bicycle expertise when working with his father. In 1971 Major moved to new premises in Smethwick and developed his own business. Today his frames and cycles are much sought after and very rare; there are only about sixty cycles known to be in existence today, and when another is found there is a buzz around enthusiasts of the marque.

Major made sure the appearance of his bikes was top quality; they were finished with high gloss paint and his trademark transfers. The major continued working, despite illness, until his death in 2005.

THE TRAM ERA

Trams and trolleybuses, like the railways in the Black Country, were developed by independent companies. They started as horse-drawn affairs, then came steam and eventually electrified trams.

Over time the different companies were brought under the auspices of the 'British Electric Traction Company', and in our region the tram system was known as the 'Black Country Tramways'. Like canals and railways, the network spread around the whole of the Black Country.

Early horse-drawn examples were in Wolverhampton by about 1878. The first route ran from Queen Square to Tettenhall and other lines went to Bilston and Willenhall. Steam trams arrived in 1881 and as early as 1887 there were experiments with an electric tramcar on the Willenhall line.

The Kinver Light Railway, built by Dudley, Stourbridge and District Electric Traction Company, was Britain's first cross-country tramway, linking Amblecote, Stourbridge (from outside the Fish Inn) with picturesque Kinver. It was possibly the best scenic tram route in the country. It replaced two one-horse carriages a day and Kinver people employed in Stourbridge no longer had a 5-mile walk to and from work.

The line opened on Good Friday 1901 and over 14,000 passengers used the service on that day. The peak of passenger numbers was recorded at about 17,000 on Whit Monday 1905.

Eventually passengers could take a through service from Birmingham, Smethwick and Dudley to Kinver. The service was unique as it ran across fields as it approached Kinver. The tram closed in 1930, one of the last services in the Black Country. The last track was taken up in 1979.

Trolleybuses had replaced trams by 1930. The tram tracks were quickly taken up, removing all signs of the tram era. Trolleybuses ran on rubber tyre wheels and required no tracks, only overhead power cables.

The pioneer of Black Country trolleybus development was a Wolverhampton man, Mr C. Owen Silvers. He converted many tram routes into trolleybus services. The era of the trolleybus lasted until almost 1970, when omnibuses replaced them.

The Parry People Mover was introduced in the mid-1980s and caused quite a stir. It was a tram made in Cradley Heath, at the end of a long line of rail engines made in the Black Country, which began in 1829 with the Foster and Rastrick engines 'Agenoria' and 'Stourbridge Lion'; and include the Kinver Light Railway.

Parry People Movers Ltd (PPML) supply lightweight tramway systems for small towns, and lightweight rail vehicles for use on regional railways. The nearest example currently in use links Stourbridge Town and Stourbridge Junction railway stations. They are highly efficient and have very low emissions. They are also very quiet.

Today Parry technologies are in use in over fifty countries around the globe. Company headquarters is still to be found in Overend Road, Cradley Heath.

BY ROAD AND BY AIR

Roads began to develop when local authorities took more responsibility in our lives. This was 'driven' by the increase in the use of cars, motorcycles and lorries.

Traffic lights for road use were first patented in the USA in 1918, but the first examples installed in England were in Wolverhampton in 1927. They were placed in Prince's Square in the middle of town, set up for a one day trial on 5 November 1927.

The road now known as the A4123 was the first 'spine' road through the Black Country. Throughout the Industrial Revolution, transport had been a vital component of what made us the 'Workshop of the World'. Turnpikes were supplemented

by canals and railways and competed for transport supremacy. Later trams and trolley buses carried people to their places of work, and then came the age of the motor car.

As road transport increased, improved attention turned to the road system. By the late 1920s cars and lorries appeared in greater numbers and challenged the canal and railroad.

On 2 November 1927 the Duke of Windsor, Prince of Wales, officially opened the Birmingham and Wolverhampton Road. As the name suggests it connected Wolverhampton with Birmingham. It also linked towns such as Dudley, Oldbury and Coseley.

The road was a feat of civil engineering; 10 miles in length and a brand new route. Seven large bridges had to be built as well as three smaller ones. The total cost was £600,000, a huge sum.

The road was not without controversy. It appealed to speeders; one coroner believed that the road was 'bewitched' with more fatalities than any he knew. In ten years he had conducted 100 inquests on people killed on the road.

Bean Industries, based in Dudley and Tipton, helped Captain Eyston achieve a speed of 357.5mph at Bonneville Salt Flats on 16 September 1938 in his car 'Thunderbolt', made by the company at Tipton. This broke the world land speed record.

The Sunbeam Motor Company was formed in Wolverhampton in 1905, but even before that they were involved in building cars. A Sunbeam 12/14 drove from Land's End to

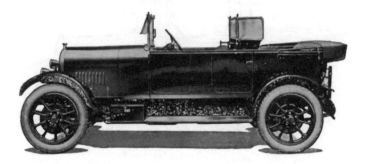

John O'Groats and back without an engine stop. The company earned a considerable reputation in the world of motoring.

The first British car to top 70mph was a Sunbeam in 1911. Between 1922 and 1927 Sunbeam held the world land speed record no fewer than five times.

Its finest hour was when Major HOD Segrave drove at a speed of 203.7 mph at Daytona Beach in Florida. Sadly, this event was the pinnacle for Sunbeam; by July 1935 it had been taken over and went out of production.

The Austin 7 car was not made in the Black Country, but many Black Country workers took the train from the bottom of Mucklow Hill in Halesowen to the Longbridge plant. An Old Hill boy called Stan Edge was one of those. He always arrived early and started work in the drawing office well before his start time of 9 a.m.

Sir Herbert Austin noticed Stan's keenness; Stan became his private draughtsman on the project at Austin's house. Only Sir Herbert and Stan were originally involved in the design. Work started in 1921 and the first Austin 7 rolled off the line in 1922.

Jensen Cars of the Lyng, West Bromwich were responsible for a number of motoring firsts. The company formed in 1934, born out of a small coach building firm, run by brothers Richard and Alan Jensen. They became one of the first manufacturers to use fibreglass bodies on their cars, and to have disk brakes on all four wheels.

In the early 1960s the C-V8 was designated one of the ugliest cars in the world. The 1966 Interceptor was described as one of the safest cars; it was the first to have all-wheel drive and anti-lock brakes. The company sadly went into liquidation in 1992, but a new company was set up in Merseyside in 1999.

Production by the new company ceased in 2002, though there are plans for another Jensen company to buy old Interceptors and completely refurbish them. Finally, watch out for an all-new Jensen, which may be built by another specialist company, so hopefully the marque will survive.

In 1957 Henry Meadows of Wolverhampton made Britain's first bubble car. It was a 'Frisky', and may have been the last mass-produced car to be produced in the town. It was made between 1958 and 1961 by a variety of companies. There were a variety of models; the cheapest was the Frisky Family Three Mk2, which cost less than £392 in 1961.

FLYING HIGH

A record balloon ascent took place over the Black Country in July 1861. James Glaisher and Henry Tracey Coxwell took off from Strafford Road Gasworks in Wolverhampton. This was the first of three flights that summer. It was a windy day, but they reached 26,000ft before landing in Rutland. A month later a second ascent reached 23,700ft and ended in Solihull.

The final flight was in early September and used a 'new'

gas that was capable of more 'lift' than on previous ascents. This time they reached at least 29,000ft. Both men began suffering oxygen deprivation, and couldn't untangle a valve line; Coxwell had to climb above the basket to untangle it.

Glaisher collapsed against the side of the basket. Both men also suffered from severe cold; their thermometer recorded a temperature of -20 Fahrenheit. Eventually Coxwell released the valve and the balloon began to descend. They landed near Ludlow.

In their report they calculated that they may have reached 36,000ft, but Glaisher had been unable to read the meters. It is accepted that they reached a height of over 30,000ft without the aid of oxygen, but almost died in the process.

25

THE HEALTH OF
THE BLACK COUNTRY

Today we take many aspects of health for granted. From our taps emerge clean, pure water. We also have a first-rate sewer system, rubbish collection and healthy and nutritious food. Our health service is the envy of the world and there are more ways to get and keep fit than you can shake a very big stick at. So, what was it like in our past? Read on.

Bilston was described as the 'Epidemic centre of the Midlands Coalfield'. When there was a cholera outbreak in 1832 a total of 742 from a total population of 14,492 died.

In 1851 a Sanitary Act Inspector, Mr Lee, held a public enquiry and surveyed the Borough of Dudley. He declared 'that this town was the worst drained and the filthiest of any town in the kingdom'.

At the time, Dudley had 28 deaths in 1,000 per annum, whereas the general average was only 20. The average life expectancy in Dudley was a paltry 16 years and 7 months, even less in poorer slum areas, such as Kates Hill.

Way before the NHS was a twinkle in Aneurin 'Nye' Bevan's eye, arrangements had to be made for people to receive medical treatment. Sick Benefit Societies were formed, including one at Dudley. It began in 1859 and by 1885 claimed to have paid out £100,000 to members. They claimed 'Healthy persons of good moral character may become members'.

John Corbett is well known for providing the Corbett Hospital at Stourbridge for the people. He bought 'The Hill', a seven bedroom mansion in 1891, refurbished it as a hospital and endowed it to the people in 1893.

Dudley Guest Hospital opened in 1867, serving around 250,000 people. A large proportion of its patients suffered from industrial diseases, as well as injuries from machinery. By 1925 it had 110 beds and fundraising events aimed to raise at least £10,000 to pay of the hospital's debt (sound familiar?). The grand finale was a giant bazaar and fayre in June, which lasted for six days.

Some 'old wives' remedies used in the Black Country are still recognised today. Here is my selection; if you try these at home it will be at your own risk. I cannot guarantee they will work, or have ever worked!

Cough Stuff – stew whole onions in brown sugar; leave hot in a basin on the hob. Ideal for children with coughs.

The Heavy Blanket – kept for sweating out fever.

The discomfort of stinging nettles can be eased by rubbing the affected part with **a dock leaf**. The two often grow together along canal towpaths and open ground.

Cold Tea (Tay) for easing 'The blight' of sore eyes.
Onions for earache and chilblains.
Linseed Meal Poultice – used to help cure boils.
Barley Water – boil barley in water and strain, used for stomach trouble.
Camomile Tea was, and still is, used as a tonic.
Human urine as an aid to complexion.

Parings of horse hoof boiled in rain water could be used for wart removal.

Tie **raw beef** near the site of toothache for 7 (or any other 'odd' number of hours).

A teaspoon of gin was given to a newborn baby to break wind.

In Old Hill cuts and grazes were treated with **'Page's ointment'**, a gritty yellow substance sold in small stone pots. **'Blue oils'** were sold in Brierley Hill to cure whooping cough.

Workers suffering from the effects of too much beer often used a hangover remedy made from **powdered snails**. I think I would rather suffer the hangover!

'**Godfrey's cordial**', made from opium and treacle, was called 'comfort' and was used as a sedative. It was even given to babies and made them go to sleep! One chemist stated he had made 20 gallons of the mix in one year.

One Black Country boy was told to get rid of a wart by tying as many knots as he could in a piece of cotton and flushing it down the toilet. He was to remain silent throughout this process. It apparently worked, the wart went and the rest of the family had a few moments peace and quiet! Another remedy involved holding a piece of raw beef on a wart. This was sometimes followed by burying the meat

Squire Knights celebrated '**Purifying Family Pills**' which had allegedly been sold for 100 years and were superior in curing indigestion and bilious complaints. Oh, and many other complaints as well ... Giddiness, headaches, cramps, fevers, sight problems and much more; ask for them at your local chemist!

Adverts for similar pills were regularly found in books such as *Curiosities of Dudley and the Black Country*. A number of glowing testimonials accompanied each advertisement. Squire Knight also made cough pills to remedy all forms of coughs and breathing problems. I wonder if any of them actually worked?

Wednesbury's own 'Bedlam' was named after the most famous one in London, founded in medieval times and short for 'Bethlehem Hospital for the Insane'. In 1821 Wednesbury Bedlam was in the High Bullen area of the town. It was in a narrow, evil smelling thoroughfare with 143 residents in 1821, from a total population in the town of 6,471.

The Bedlam name was attached to a variety of similar hospitals around the country. Wednesbury Bedlam lasted until the 1870s, conditions were harsh and residents labelled as 'imbecile', 'idiotic' or 'insane'. Treatment included ice-cold baths and opium, both thought to calm people down. This inhuman treatment changed in the 1860s, when attitudes towards mental illness changed.

Children's employment caused concern in the nineteenth century. Parliament set up an enquiry in 1840 to look at the conditions that children were working under in South Staffordshire and other areas; their findings are startling:

> 13-year-old Enoch, who works with his father, is said to be excessively stupid and unconcerned, not clean and not well clothed.
>
> 15-year-old John is an apprentice who has enough to eat. His master only beats him for going out without leave. He has no wages; he cannot read or write and is disagreeable [he smelt!]
>
> 7-year-old Rebecca is left all day (from 6am-6pm) to look after her five year old sister, sometimes she plays hide and seek among the cinder banks.

Other children were assaulted with ropes, made to work for up to 14 hours a day and often carried out heavy work. Conditions were poor at work in many cases, with boys feeling the effect of chemical dust. Clothing was regularly poor, children had little or no education and their food was meagre.

It is little wonder that the average mortality rate in the region was as low as 21!

26

BLACK COUNTRY INDUSTRY

It is very difficult to write an anthology of Black Country facts without referring to facts about manufacturing and industry. It played such an important part in our history and heritage. I hope you enjoy my selection of facts about industry.

This short poem has often been used to conjure up an image of what it was like during the Industrial Revolution:

When Satan stood on Brierley Hill
And far around him gazed
He said, 'I never shall again
At Hell's flames be amazed'
He staggered on to Dudley Woodside
And there he laid him down and died.

Quarrying took place in the Black Country as early as 1272 in Sedgley, at Kingswinford in 1291 and Wednesbury in 1315. They began to find and mine 'pit-cole'. These 'delvers' as they were called, became charcoal burners and early smiths, using charcoal to smelt local iron.

Dud Dudley was born about 1600, the illegitimate son of Edward Sutton, the fifth Baron Dudley. In his book *Metallum Martis*, first published in 1665, Dud claimed his great invention. He was described as the first: 'Artificer in Iron made with pit coale and sea coale in 1618'. He sought to invent a method of smelting iron from coal rather than charcoal. After a couple of experiments he found: 'The quality to be good and profitable.'

There was much jealousy of Dud's invention from other ironmasters, and they pursued him legally. It seemed Dud was tactless and provoked them at every turn. He was also unlucky in that his forge and equipment at Cradley was swept away by floods down the Stour. Dud's furnace at Sedgley was also attacked by rivals.

One of the oldest companies in Britain is located in the Black Country, according to the *Financial Times* (1992), who published a list of the oldest companies. At number 21 in the list is the Folkes Group at Lye, Stourbridge, established in 1699. Top of the list is Aberdeen Harbour Board, established in 1136.

In 1981 history was made when a member of the ninth generation of the Folkes dynasty, Constantine Folkes, became the youngest Chairman of a listed PLC at the age of 28. In 2002 Folkes was still one of the largest private companies in the West Midlands. It continues to own one of the largest open die forges in Europe (Somers Forge Ltd, Halesowen) as well as two metal heat treatment companies at Lye and Cradley Heath.

Somers Forge has more than a century of experience, first founded on Mucklow Hill by Walter Somers in 1866. Not without controversy, it was involved in the 1980s 'Arms-for-Iraq' scandal. It is a major exporter to the USA, with a 10,000 square feet warehouse in Detroit.

Thomas Newcomen made the first successful atmospheric steam pumping engine, and located it 'somewhere at Coneygre' near Tipton in 1712. This was where some of the earliest commercial coal mining took place. Water was the scourge of mining, and Newcomen's engine was the first to help tackle the situation.

Newcomen came from Dartmouth in Devon. There is a recently refurbished replica of his engine at the Black Country Living Museum and another model at Dartmouth.

Thomas Savery was another inventor of steam engines, and a business partner of Newcomen. In 1739 one of his engines was erected at Broad Waters near Wednesbury. It failed due to flooding in the mine. The quantity of steam raised was so great as to 'rent the whole machine to pieces'.

In 1760 William Salter started business in Bilston making a portable weighing device. This was the start of a huge enterprise. The company later moved to West Bromwich and, as well as making all varieties of springs, they also made

bayonets during the period of the Indian Mutiny and the American Civil War.

In the 1960s they were making upwards of 500,000 springs, as well as weighing scales. The company was also responsible for making the first typewriters in the Black Country.

One of Walsall's early manufacturing industries was lorinry; loriners also made shoe buckles in great numbers. In 1792 fashion started to change and slippers and shoestrings became popular. A deputation was sent to the Prince of Wales to support the use of buckles on shoes, and to give up the new fashion. This fell on deaf ears and by 1820 the buckle trade was in decline. By this time the leather making industry had started to flourish and the town survived and thrived.

Birmingham has traditionally been associated as a centre of gun making, but I must point out that there is a gun making tradition in the Black Country. Wednesbury was famed for making gun barrels, Walsall made gun stocks and Darlaston made gun locks. They were then often shipped to Birmingham where they were assembled and then stamped 'Made in Birmingham'.

Eliza Tinsley was a rare women business owner in the nineteenth century. She was a chain maker with factories in Old Hill and Cradley Heath, and her company made the longest mine chain ever produced. Eliza was born into a nail making family, her husband was a nail factor, Thomas Tinsley, and when he died in 1851 she took over the company and ran it for twenty years.

Tinsley's owned warehouses across the region and was considered to be the largest company of its kind in Staffordshire. In 1871 4,000 were employed and the firm boasted it could supply any type of nail. In 1872 Eliza retired and sold the business. The company exists today; it was acquired by the Atlantic Group in 2006.

Most Black Country folk will remember Round Oak, 'The Earl's'. It was a company that helped defined the area as the major industrial region during the Industrial Revolution. But what was there before Round Oak?

In 1786 Messrs Croft built a blast furnace at The Level, Brierley Hill. By the early nineteenth century the Gibbons family enlarged the business. Later the Ward family stepped in, and from 1857 the history of Round Oak began.

The 2nd Lord Dudley was granted the right to cut down all the timber around the area and he established a timber yard and wharf on Dudley Canal so he could transport lumber, which was in great demand. Round Oak then followed and today the land is part of the Merry Hill Centre.

It became a steelworks in the 1890s, when the Bessemer process for making mild steel brought about the decline of the wrought iron industry. Round Oak closed in 1980, a huge blow to the town of Brierley Hill.

Another major iron and steel works began as Hickman's Ironworks in Bilston. It was described in the 1930s as 'Bilston Illuminations', and housed the most famous furnace, installed in 1954 and christened 'Elisabeth' after the daughter of the company chairman.

By the early 1970s Elisabeth was the last blast furnace in operation in the Black Country. In 1980 it was demolished, ending well over 200 years of Black Country blast furnace operations.

There were Black Country links to the Festival of Britain in 1951, fifty years before the Millennium Dome was built in London. Black Country firms were heavily involved in the construction of another domed building to be erected in the city.

The 1951 Festival was held on the South Bank of the Thames. Companies that built the dome, as well as other buildings, were Horseley Bridge and Thomas Pigott of Tipton. The dome was erected by Carter Horseley (Engineers) Ltd, and 232 tons of aluminium and 133 tons of steel were used; the total cost of materials and erection was £183,000.

The first company in the world to recycle plastic from mixed plastics was Wolverhampton-based Omnia Recycling in 2008.

BLACK COUNTRY GOODS FAR AND WIDE

In 1867 Wrights of Dudley supplied 11,000 anvils to the USA.

In 1919 Braithwaite and Kirk of West Bromwich supplied sixty small span bridges to Uganda.

A Wednesbury-made railway turntable was found recently in Israel. It was found at the Israeli Defence Forces History Museum in Jaffa. This was made by the Metropolitan Carriage, Waggon and Finance Co. at the Old Park Works in Wednesbury in 1921.

Groves Button Works in Halesowen were the largest button manufacturer in England. They sold their products worldwide, including supplying both sides in the American Civil War with uniform buttons. Sadly, the company closed in 2012.

Linda Button, who lived in Halesowen some years ago, once received an order for a large quantity of military uniform buttons. The order included design drawings. This was returned to sender with a tongue-in-cheek letter.

The manufacture of ramrods used during the American wars was celebrated in the names Ramrod Hall, Ramrod Colliery and Ramrod Hall Brickworks. These were all situated in Rowley around Whiteheath.

WHO MADE WHAT?

Benjamin Mander founded the famous family business bearing his name in 1773. His son Charles steered the business towards paint when, in 1817, he went on the road to sell Mander varnish. He travelled to Bristol and on to Bridgwater to drum up trade. He initially succeeded in selling two quarts to the son of a coach maker, and the rest, as they say was history.

Mander Paints expanded to include paint, lacquer and pigments, and they were famous for their japanned work as

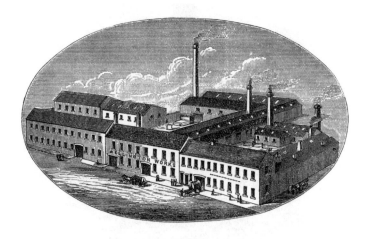

well as manufacturing other chemicals. In the 1990s Manders PLC was one of Europe's largest manufacturers and distributors of publishing and industrial inks. The Mander Shopping Centre in Wolverhampton was named after the family.

Why does Sedgley Coat of Arms have two nibs on it? The answer is simple; the town was an important centre in pen-making history. Pen manufacture began in the late eighteenth century. There are records of Daniel Fellows of Sedgley making steel pens in 1800, and also of Fellows and an apprentice, Thomas Sheldon, making steel pens in 1806.

Who was the first to make steel pens was the subject of controversy. Daniel Fellows made that claim in a pamphlet in 1805, but counter–claims followed. There are no records of any building in Sedgley where pens were made, but there was a pen factory in Zoar Street, Gornal, where pen making was carried out until the 1950s.

Chance Brothers Glassworks in Smethwick dates back to 1814. In 1832 it was the first company in England to make sheet glass and the only company for about fifty years to make optical glass. In 1851 it made 1¼ million square feet of glass for the Crystal Palace and the Great Exhibition.

R. pearson

Chances also made prism lenses for lighthouses, including the Longstone Lighthouse in Northumberland. This is where Grace Darling lived, the heroine who in 1838 spotted the wreck of the *Forfarshire* on Big Harcar, a low rocky island. She conducted an amazing rescue of survivors with her father, battling gale force winds and huge waves to do so.

The lens of the lighthouse is on display at 'Thinktank' at Millennium Point in Birmingham. The company also supplied the prism for the southernmost lighthouse in the world at Leeuwin Point, in Australia.

John Spencer, an Ironmaster of the Phoenix Ironworks, Spon Lane in West Bromwich, invented corrugated iron, purely by accident, in 1844.

Long-established company Rubery Owen gained a reputation as structural engineers. Founded in the late nineteenth century, they made products locally for projects further afield. Two examples are Wembley Stadium (the one that was recently replaced) and Oxford Circus underground station.

Today they are still family owned and based in Darlaston. At their height they employed 17,000 people worldwide. Many of the cars on the road in history will have had parts made by Rubery Owen.

The Jew's Harp is the most simple of musical instruments. Many were made in Rowley Regis. Another company in Netherton exported thousands to North America where, it is said, they were among the trinkets or offerings given to Native Americans to purchase land. There is also evidence in 1900 of production in a small Blackheath workshop.

J. Bristow, from Willenhall, invented a 'bump machine' to test car radios. In the early 1950s car radios were popular, but they suffered problems with reception because of the rattles and bumps synonymous with old cars. The machine was invented in Bristow's own small factory in his back yard. The company who commissioned this vital piece of equipment would later become Decca.

Ninety per cent of the locks, latches and keys produced in the UK were made in Willenhall by the late 1950s.

R. pearson

The maker of the Queen's handbag for her Italian visit in 2000 was Launer London, whose factory is in Walsall. Sam Launer came from Czechoslovakia over sixty years ago and was awarded the Royal Warrant in 1981 for handbags and small leather goods to the Queen.

Walsall firm S. MacNeillie and Son converted three James Bond-style cars for Tony Blair. The contract was won in 2003 for three Jaguar Limousines to have £200,000 worth of additional security features added to protect the then prime minister.

THE WORKERS

There were employers, factory owners, factories and other businesses. None of these would have lasted long without the most important element: the worker. Work was almost always physically difficult and often dangerous. Here are a few of the jobs carried out:

A **page** in brickmaking was often a girl. She was a brick moulder's labourer and could carry around 15 tons of clay a day. By 1850 Stourbridge alone was making some 14 million bricks a year.

A **brow girl** was a female pithead worker.

A **rolleyway man** maintained the underground railway in the mines.

A **throstle spinner** operated a throstle machine which continually wound and twisted wool or cotton fibres in the textile industry.

Nineteenth-century Black Country saltmen from Ruiton were known as hawkers. A hawker usually worked with his wife. Their cart had two large wheels and a frame covered with

tarpaulin to keep the salt dry. An example of a salt cart is exhibited at the Black Country Living Museum.

The salt trade ran from March to November, with early morning starts. The couple first collected their salt from a depot in Dudley and then set about selling it far and wide across the region. Sales of blocks of salt were mainly to shops, smaller blocks went to big houses.

All the salt carried had to be sold, so the working day was long. Sellers sometimes slept overnight in a field or under the tarpaulin, so they could sell the rest of their load the following day.

The trade died out in the twentieth century when crushed salt started to be sold. Wholesalers began offering credit to shopkeepers, which finished off the trade totally.

The 1879 depression in the Black Country affected prices and wages, and levels of employment slumped dramatically. Many miners were reduced to working two or three days a week. The winter of 1878–1879 was also exceptionally severe, which led to mass unemployment in the iron, coal and hardware trades.

The workhouses saw an increase in out-door relief and many more people were forced into the workhouse. There was a decrease in school attendance because pupils had no clothes and no food. Black despair sat over the Black Country.

27

SPORT

FOOTBALL CLUBS

Black Country England Internationals – Top Ten

1. **Jesse Pennington**: was born in West Bromwich, but played his whole career at Blackburn Rovers. He won 25 England caps between 1907 and 1920.

2. **Bert Williams**: a great goalkeeper who played for Wolves. Bert was born at Bilston and started his career at Walsall. He won 24 caps between 1949 and 1955.

3= This position is tied between two players, each on 23 caps.
   Steve Bloomer: a Cradley lad and the first player to score a goal at the Hawthorns during the ground's inaugural match. Steve earned his caps between 1895 and 1907.
   Don Howe: born in Wolverhampton and played for Albion and Arsenal, he later managed Albion and the England team. Don earned his caps between 1957 and 1959.

5. **Allan Clarke**: born in Willenhall, he began his career at Walsall, and then played for Fulham and Leicester before finding fame at Leeds United. He earned a total of 19 caps.

6= This position is tied between three players, each on 18 caps:
   Duncan Edwards, he earned his caps between 1955 and 1957; **Billy Walker,** a Wednesbury-born Aston Villa player earned his caps between 1920 and 1932; and **Carlton Palmer,** the last Black Country-born player to regularly play league football. Carlton was born in Rowley Regis, and was a YTS player at Albion before moving to Sheffield Wednesday.

9. **Billy Bassett**: the Albion winger with three FA Cup final appearances before 1900. Earned 16 caps between 1888 and 1896.
10. **Steve Bull**: Tipton-born hero of the Wolves, began his career with the Baggies. He earned 13 caps between 1989 and 1990.

TOP TOWNS FOR
ENGLAND-BORN INTERNATIONALS

Wolverhampton – 10 players
West Bromwich – 9 players
Walsall – 8 players
Wednesbury – 3 players
Tipton – 2 players

Walsall FC
Walsall came into being as a result of the amalgamation of 'working-class' Walsall Swifts and the 'posh' Walsall Town. They became a founder member of the second division in 1892 and play at Bescot Stadium, which was opened in 1990 by Stanley Matthews. Previously they were at Fellows Park, originally known as Hilary Street, but it is now a Morrison's supermarket.

The record attendance at Fellows Park was 25,453 for a match against Newcastle United in 1961. The Bescot record is 11,049, against Rotherham in 2004. That said, the new stadium only seats 11,300.

Record victory: 10–0 against Darwen in 1899.

Record defeat: 0–12 against Small Heath in 1892 and also against Darwen in 1896.

West Bromwich Albion
West Bromwich Strollers formed in 1879, the following year they became West Bromwich Albion. Their nickname 'The Baggies' came from the fact that their supporters were ironworkers who wore moleskin trousers held up with belts.

They occasionally hitched up their trousers, which began to sag over their boots. There are alternative explanations of how they acquired this nickname, and I cannot find any conclusive evidence one way or another.

The Baggies have won the FA Cup in 1888, 1892, 1931, 1954 and 1968.

WBA moved to their ground 'The Hawthorns' in 1900. The ground was common-land with many hawthorn bushes, populated with many thrushes, also known as 'throstles'. This probably led to their other nickname.

The Albion ground is the highest in Britain, some 551ft (168m) above sea level. It was the last football league ground to be built in the nineteenth century.

WBA were the first European professional side to play in China in 1978, and the first professional side to win a match in the Soviet Union in 1957.

Jeff Astle, 'King of the Hawthorns' played five games for England.

Wolverhampton Wanderers
Wolves were one of the twelve founder members of the Football League in 1888. They have won the FA Cup three times in 1893, 1908 and 1949.

In the mid-1950s the Wolves were described as 'Champions of the World' by the *Daily Mail*. They played in a series of friendly games against such august opposition as Moscow Dynamo, Real Madrid and Borussia Dortmund. In the process they became the first English team to play in the Soviet Union.

Overseas exploits continued into the 1960s, with a Wolves team competing in a North American league called the 'United Soccer Association'; comprising twelve teams from Europe and South America. The 'Los Angeles Wolves' won the Western Division and then won the league title after beating 'Washington Whips' (Aberdeen) in the final championship match.

Billy Wright of Wolves was the first player in history to win 100 full caps; his hundredth was England *v.* Scotland at Wembley in 1959.

BLACK COUNTRY GOLF CLUBS

Dudley Golf Club was founded in 1893, a hilly parkland course

Sandwell Park was founded in 1895 as West Bromwich Golf Club, an inland links course.

The South Staffordshire Golf Club near Wolverhampton was founded in 1892 and moved to Tettenhall in 1908.

Halesowen Golf Club was founded in 1906. The clubhouse was once the home of William Shenstone.

Walsall Golf Club was founded in 1907, a parkland course.

Penn Golf Club was founded in 1908 on Penn Common.

Dartmouth Golf Club in West Bromwich boasts the longest opening hole in Europe, a 675 yard par 5.

Bloxwich Golf Club opened in 1923, a semi-parkland course. The first player to score a hole-in-one was Major R.W. Downs in 1925.

Swindon Golf Club is a parkland course, which opened in 1974 as Blackhills. It changed its name in 1986.

Brandhall Golf Course can be found at Oldbury and is a woodland course.

Wergs Golf Club at Tettenhall is owned and run by the Moseley family. It opened in 1990 and is the longest course in Staffordshire.

Walsall Golf Club has links to Augusta National in Georgia, where the Masters is played each year. By May 1907 it had 123 members, but it was August before the first ball was struck.

Prominent golf course designer, Dr Alistair Malcolm, was paid £1,000 plus expenses to increase the size of the course from 14 to 18 holes, the work itself cost £2,000. Malcolm's career in golf club design was impressive; he was responsible for the Augusta National, Royal Melbourne and Cypress Point courses.

Dudley Golf Club opened as a links course. In April 1927 a new 18-hole course was completed. If one was introduced by a member the charge for a round of golf in 1927 was 2' 6" (12½p), a weekly rate was 10s (50p). This rate was for the links course, not the new one.

RUGBY

Wolverhampton had one of the first rugby clubs in the country, founded in 1875. It met initially in the 'Star and Garter' pub in Wolverhampton. Early matches were at Tettenhall Road, near the 'Halfway House', they also played at West Park and other places before settling in Castlecroft in 1950.

Wednesday Rugby Club has the highest goalposts in the world. When the club moved in 2004 it was decided to go for the record, which they achieved with a height of 38.26m. Prior to this, Old Halesonians held the UK record at 22.15m.

Dudley Kingswinford Rugby Club hails to the time immediately after the First World War Harper, Sons and Bean, makers of the Bean car. In 1923 the club changed its name to Bean Football Club and a year later Dudley Rugby Football Club. Soon after 'Kingswinford' was added to the name.

Other Rugby clubs in the Black Country include Warley, Old Halesonians, Wednesbury, Walsall and Stourbridge.

SPEEDWAY

Cradley Heathens speedway had the most British National speedway Knockout Cup wins – eight by 1992. But at the end of the 1994 season, the future of the Dudley Wood stadium looked bleak. They managed to hang on there for the 1995 season before Barratt's built a housing estate on the stadium site.

The Heathens then played 'home' matches at Stoke, using the name 'Cradley and Stoke' Heathens. The team still competes in the National League as Dudley Heathens and their home matches are shared between Monmore Green at Wolverhampton, and Perry Barr in Birmingham.

The search for a new ground, and a return to the name 'Cradley Heathens', continues.

SPORTING LEGENDS

Jack Holden was a Tipton Harrier and achieved great success in a career lasting over thirty years. He was three times English Cross Country Champion from 1933–35, and ran with the English Cross Country team nine times between 1929 and 1946.

He represented his country in the 1934 and 1950 Empire Games and finally retired from running in 1951. He died in Bradley, Bilston in March 2004, six days before his 97th birthday.

Dudley's Dorothy Round was England's number one lawn tennis player in the late 1930s and twice Women's World Tennis Champion. She was born in Park Road (now Parkway Road), Dudley, and continued to live in Dudley in her later years.

Dorothy was lucky in that her home had its own private tennis court. She had a simple motto when it came to tennis: 'always play with someone better than yourself'. In later life, Dorothy became a county golf and hockey player.

Charles Henry Palmer was a Cricketing Legend who played for Old Hill Cricket Club, which has produced some of the finest cricketers in England. In 1948 he scored 85 whilst playing for Worcestershire against the Australian tourists.

In 1955 Palmer carried out a remarkable feat while playing for Leicestershire against Surrey, one of the strongest batting line–ups in the country. Medium–pace bowler Palmer took eight wickets for no runs, his final figure was eight wickets for seven runs from 14 overs, 12 of those overs were maidens.

Palmer became a master at Bromsgrove School, teaching English whilst playing County Cricket. From 1938 to 1949 he played for Worcestershire and also played in one test–match, against the West Indies in Barbados during the 1953–54 series.

Palmer was President of the MCC in 1978–79 as well as being Chairman of both the Cricket Council and the Test and Country Cricket Board. He died on 31 March 2005, aged 85.

Don Bradman's batting record was foiled by Black Country bowler Eric Hollies in the 1948 Test Series between England and Australia. In the fifth Test Match at the Oval, cricketing legend Bradman came to the crease for his last test cricket innings for Australia. Bradman needed only 4 runs to achieve a test average of 100 runs per innings.

Step up Hollies, the Old Hill-born Black Country cricketer. As Bradman faced Hollies, John Arlott commented: 'Two slips, a silly mid-off and a short leg close to him as Hollies pitches the ball up slowly and ... he's bowled'. Bradman had been bowled second ball for nought.

Smethwick-born bowler Sydney Francis Barnes (1873–1967) is regarded as one of the greatest bowlers in cricket history. Barnes was unusual because he only spent two seasons in first-class cricket, preferring to play league cricket and represent Staffordshire in the Minor Counties.

Barnes played for the county until he was 61. In Test cricket, Barnes played for England twenty-seven times from 1901 to 1914, taking 189 wickets. He is ranked first in the ICC Best-Ever Test Championship Rating for bowlers.

In 1911–12, Barnes enabled England to win The Ashes when he took 34 wickets in the series. In 1913–14, his final Test series, he took a world record 49 wickets against South Africa. In 1963, Barnes was named one of 'Six Giants of the Wisden Century', and later inducted into the ICC Cricket Hall of Fame.

Tessa Sanderson MBE, from Wednesfield, was the only British athlete to compete at five Olympic Games. She competed for the first time in 1976, when she came tenth in her event, the javelin. She was Olympic Champion in 1984, and she came fourth in her last Games in 1992.

The first ever world lightweight boxing champion was Abraham Hichen (born in Wolverhampton). Hichen emigrated to USA and won the title over there in 1868.

Dave Heeley, better known as 'Blind Dave' from West Bromwich, was the third ever man to run seven marathons on seven continents in seven days. He did this for charity in 2008. He is the first blind man to achieve the feat.

Steve Bloomer, Cradley-born footballer, scored 28 goals in 23 games for England, a record for an England player at the time. His scoring rate of 74 minutes per goal has only been equalled by one player, his contemporary Vivian Woodward. When he was a Derby player he scored 331 goals in 524 matches, a club record that still stands.

Bloomer's last England goal was scored in 1907, against the 'auld-enemy', Scotland. Bloomer was also famous for being the only Cradley (or Black Country) player to be mentioned in the works of P.G. Wodehouse in a short story: *The Goalkeeper and the Plutocrat*. Bloomer has a memorial plaque at

Bridge Street, Cradley, where he was born in 1874.

George Henry Holden played football for Wednesbury Old Athletic and England. He was the first West Bromwich man to play for England, the first Black Country man to play for England and the last footballer to play for his country while playing for a Wednesbury team. In March 1881 George played his first full match for England against Scotland at the Kensington Oval, London.

The 'Staffie' or Staffordshire Bull Terrier was first recognised as a pedigree dog in 1935. The breed itself is much older, it just took the Kennel Club a while to find it. The Staffie was originally bred as a sports dog.

The 'sports' for which it was bred were bull baiting, dog fighting and other blood sports, banned in 1835 but continued underground for years afterwards. The Hertfordshire Open Show on 20 June 1935 was first to post classes for Stafford's.

The first meeting of the Staffordshire Bull Terrier Club took place at the Old Cross Guns pub in Cradley Heath in July 1935. On 17 August 1935 the Staffordshire Bull Terrier Club held its first show at Cradley Heath. It made its first appearance at Crufts in 1936.

Bull-baiting and cock-fighting in Walsall became such a problem that the constables threatened pub licensees that if they encouraged the sports, or assisted in cock fighting then their licence would be taken from them. After 1835 anyone guilty of providing a room or place for such 'sport' could be fined up to £5. This law was more or less ignored until the early 1900s.

Rat pits were another Black Country spectacle. A dog was put in a pit with thirty rats. The pit was a small cage and the winner was the dog that killed most rats in a given time. There was often heavy betting on the result. Oldbury was one centre for this 'sport'.

LOCAL SPORT PERSONALITIES

William Perry was the Tipton Slasher, Champion of England from 1850–1857. At this time boxing was brutal! Perry had a slashing method of boxing, hence his nickname. He fought his largest and probably most difficult opponent in December 1842. Charles Freeman, the 'American Giant', was 6ft 9in tall and weighed 275lb (125kg).

Bareknuckle fighting was illegal. However, in Regency England, the law was regularly ignored. The fight against Freeman ran for 38 rounds. The result was disqualification for the 'Slasher', having allegedly fallen to the ground without being punched.

Perry's last fight was in June 1857 when he lost to Tom Sayers. This fight broke him as he had bet just about his whole worth on the fight and subsequently became penniless. He began working on the canals again and became a heavy drinker.

Perry died in 1880 and was buried in the churchyard of St Johns in Kates Hill. In 1993 a memorial statue commemorating William Perry was unveiled in the Coronation Gardens in Owen Street, Tipton.

Jumping Joe Darby, known locally as 'Jose the jumper' set a world record for five forward spring jumps with weights at Dudley Castle. The total distance he jumped was 76ft 3ins. In November 1888 Darby did his own Royal Command Performance at a restaurant in Covent Garden before the Prince of Wales and other members of the Royal Family.

In 1972 John Swallow, ATV reporter, tried to emulate another of Joe's jumping feats, when he tried to jump a canal from a standing jump, including landing on the water without breaking the surface. Needless to say he failed in his effort, unlike Joe. There is a statue in the centre of Netherton commemorating Darby.

28

THE ECLECTIC BLACK COUNTRY

A Wolverhampton man, Button Gwinnett, signed the American Declaration of Independence. Gwinnett and his wife, Ann, moved to Georgia in 1765 and started a plantation. There is a blue plaque near to St Peter's in Wolverhampton celebrating Gwinnett.

Gwinnett became a prominent figure and voted in favour of the Declaration of Independence. On the original document his signature was the second to be added to the document.

His autograph is one of the most valuable in the world and Isaac Asimov celebrated it in a short story 'Button, Button'. There are only fifty-one known examples of his signature in existence, hence its value.

A donkey, a pig and a goose caused a riot at the Theatre Royal in Wolverhampton in about 1844. The animals had been

brought into the theatre to take part in a performance, being quartered beneath the stage. The following morning all that was left of the goose were some feathers, it had been eaten by the pig. Next morning the donkey was dead with teeth marks on its legs, it was assumed the pig had bitten it, causing it to run upstairs, but it fell and died.

The show went on, but when it came to the part where the donkey and goose were to be on stage, an announcement was made to the audience. They did not take the news well. Benches were torn up and thrown and there was a free-for-all. The curtain had to come down prematurely on the show.

Wolverhampton Morris Dancers were prevented from their seasonal custom by Oliver Cromwell's Puritans in 1652. Some young people set up a maypole, but were summonsed to appear before justices. They stated they were celebrating the dissolution of Parliament but a deeper, more sinister plot was suspected. A minor riot took place against the Parliament, requiring troops to quell the unrest.

The following was written in the Manorial Rolls in about 1833. It relates to Elizabeth Waltho from Stowheath and is a good example of the reason why the Plain English Society was set up.

> To this court came Elizabeth Rhodes of Woodsetton in the parish of Sedgley [you need to concentrate here] widow before her marriage with her late husband Thomas Rhodes Elizabeth Walters otherwise known as Waltho spinster one of the two sisters and co-heiresses of Edward Walters [their brother] otherwise Waltho deceased who was only son and heir of Edward Walters otherwise Waltho deceased who was only son and heir of Edward Walters heretofore of the Lodge in the parish of Sedgley long since deceased.

Walsall had Public Baths in Littleton Street between the 1860s and 1890s. The water came from Elias Crapper's Lime Pit and was very cold and very green. The admission rate depended on the density of filth in the water.

A small part of Coseley was called 'Sodom', probably because of the behaviour of its inhabitants. It became acceptable in time, enough to appear on the deeds of a Mission church, connected with the parish of St Mary.

One of 'Iron-mad' Wilkinson's more eclectic projects was the Cast Iron Chapel. Early Methodists in Bradley begged him to build them a chapel and he agreed. Wilkinson declared that as much of the chapel as possible should be made from iron, including windows, pillars and pulpit, nails and hinges, door steps, roof ties and supports. All that is left today is the pulpit.

In Wednesbury stands St Bartholomew's Church. It has a most unusual feature; the lectern sports a fighting cock, instead of the more traditional eagle. The cock has spurs and a shaven comb and is about 400 years old, when cock fighting was a popular sport.

Before the days of online dating, Black Country girls used other methods to find a mate. On the first showing of a new moon a girl might turn her innermost garment when she went to bed, reciting:

New moon show to me
Who my true love shall be

And in her sleep, it is said; she would see an image of her future husband.

Black Country people believed the sun danced on Easter Monday. Large crowds gathered in the early morning to watch the spectacle. This belief was shared with the Irish and many European countries, who believed that on Easter Sunday the sun dances with joy that the Saviour is risen.

A Walsall mum has three sons, each one born on the same day of the year. Lillian Green, churchman's wife, created her own special Holy Trinity when she gave birth on the 6th of March in 1978, 1980 and 1983.

In 1354 Wolverhampton was granted the right to hold annual wool fairs. The town was then a busy market place for the sale of wool and traders came from all over, including Europe. In July there were celebrations to St Blaise, the patron saint of wool-combers. The great and the good attended an early service, followed by a procession 'walking the fair', involving merchants and locals.

The procession ended at High Green (now Queen Square), followed by much carousing. This lasted between eight days and two weeks, ending with a night of music, dancing, singing and drinking.

In 1684 at Rowley Church a tenor bell was given by William Stavenor. It bore the legend: 'My roaring sound doth warning give that men cannot alwayes live'.

Betty Boothroyd MP famously wrote in her autobiography that Queen Victoria ordered the curtains of her carriage in the Royal Train to be closed as she passed through West Bromwich on her way to Manchester.

Betty was originally from Yorkshire. She held several constituencies before becoming West Bromwich MP in 1973. In 1992 she became Speaker of the House of Commons and was given a life peerage as Baroness Boothroyd of Sandwell in 2001. Betty is a supporter of West Bromwich Albion.

Former Prime Minister John Major has Black Country roots. His father, Tom, was born in Bloxwich and became a member of Walsall Swimming Club. The family surname was actually Ball, but Tom adopted the name Major. John was christened John Major-Ball.

Major has a further link to the midlands; his wife Norma was born at Much Wenlock in Shropshire. Both Tom and John's grandfather, John Ball, were locksmiths in Willenhall. In 1992 Prime Minister Major accepted honorary membership of the Friends of Willenhall Lock Museum.

Tipton was home to Bonzo the ape who was tried for manslaughter. Jack Jevons owned Bonzo and matched him in a bare fist fight with Josiah Smith, a pretender to the

Tipton Slasher title. Smith was so badly maimed that he died of his injuries a few days after the fight. Bonzo was tried at Wednesbury and sentenced to have his teeth drawn.

In the 1920s workmen digging in the western end of Victoria Park, Darlaston were surprised when the ground gave way beneath them. They fell into the cellars of the former Darlaston House, where they found, still intact and drinkable, several bottles of wine. The workmen drank the lot and there was no more work done that day!

What's a Tiswas? No, not the Saturday morning TV show with Lenny Henry. During nailers riots in the Lye the rioters developed a deterrent to fend off the mounted militia. They made a four-pointed star which was thrown on the floor and always landed with one spike facing up.

They were given the name TISWAS, which stands for 'It is as it was'. Of course, military historians know that the TISWAS is not a Black Country invention, the Romans used them in battle and they were called caltrops.

Who Put the Pig on the Wall in Gornal? One explanation is that Teddy Turner's butcher shop had a grassed paddock in front, where he held livestock he couldn't accommodate in his slaughterhouse. The paddock was walled with Gornal stone.

It is believed that one Johnny Longstomach put the pig on the wall surrounding the paddock, but how true is that? I have seen a photograph of the phenomenon, so maybe it is fact. There was a pub in Gornal called 'The Pig on the Wall' but it's now a McDonald's.

Weddings often provide great opportunities for 'upstaging' and 'upman (or woman) ship'. In 1949 one event in Tipton, described as a Tipton Wedding with a difference, was difficult to top.

Joan Hodgkiss married Lawrence Garner at Owen Street Church. When the happy couple emerged from the ceremony they were not whisked away in an open-top Rolls-Royce, nor was there a horse-drawn carriage to romantically transport them to their reception. No, their chosen mode of travel was a pair of elephants. One of the elephants knelt down for the couple to climb aboard.

Why elephants? It may come as no surprise to hear there was a link to nearby Dudley Zoo; Joan was a manageress there and it just felt right! It probably saved the couple some money as well.

A piece of Black Country History is now located in Stratford-on-Avon. In 1596 Denis Bradley built Bradley Hall, on the site of an earlier house with the same name, from 1526. The Hall was sold at auction in February 1924, then dismantled and re-erected at Tiddington Road, Stratford-upon-Avon in 1924-5, where it is known as Bradley Lodge.

The price paid for this Elizabethan Mansion House plus 15 acres of land was £2,775. Further investigation of this unusual 'house move' was carried out and a 2005 survey of Tiddington Road suggests that materials from Bradley Hall were used in the construction of four houses, including No. 64. The houses were built in 1924–25.

What links the Black Country and Tipperary? The link is Jack Judge. Jack was of Irish descent and his parents moved to Low Town in Oldbury. Jack was born in 1872. He started a business aged just 14, as a fishmonger, and was also a regular theatre performer.

In 1910 whilst appearing at the Grand Theatre in Stalybridge, Jack was challenged to a 5s wager to write and sing a song in one day. Jack won the bet with 'It's a Long Way to Tipperary'. His song lifted the hearts of those on active service during the world wars. Tipperary became so popular that Jack was paid £5 per week for life in lieu of royalties. Jack died in 1938 and is buried at Rood End in West Bromwich.

Prior to writing 'Tipperary' Judge had a recording career. In January 1915 he recorded at HMV Studios in Middlesex, and also recorded for Columbia. 'Tipperary' marked the climax of his career, but was the concluding event in his recording career. Jack had one further attempt at recording; in November 1929 he recorded 'You're all the Better For That', released on the Metropole label.

Aristotle Tump was author of a number of Black Country books published some years ago. As you may have guessed this was a nom de plume; the writer was, in fact, Harry Taylor, founder of the long-running *Black Country Bugle* newspaper.

An interesting census entry saw Catherine Mitchell described as 'The bible woman' for her occupation in the 1871 census. She sold bibles and travelled up to 20 miles a day around the Black Country, working very long hours to sell her bibles. The number of such occupations around the country in the census is in single figures.

The copy of the Portland Vase made by John Northwood in the 1870s was the most expensive glass item in the world. It sold in 1975 for £30,000. The latest project to create replicas of the Portland Vase was completed in 2012 at Stourbridge Glass Engravers in the Ruskin Centre, Stourbridge, the work of Ian Dury, the owner of the company, with engraving by Terri Colledge. The vase and its companions have not yet been formally valued, but like the credit card advert on TV, are probably 'priceless'.

Lady Godiva, famed for her naked ride through Coventry, possessed the Manor of Lower Penn, according to chronicler 'Ingulphus'. She was a powerful woman in her time and owned lands across the midlands. Godiva is the Latin form of the Anglo-Saxon name Godgifu, or 'Gift of God'.

The legend of her naked ride is probably false. It was first chronicled in 1236, two centuries after Godiva's death.

Ingulphus was Arthur Gray who was the 'Master of Jesus College' early in the twentieth century.

One of the few woman newspaper owners in the country was Kathleen Billingsley. She owned the *Smethwick Telephone* from 1943 until her death in 1962.

The inventor of the mass spectrograph was Francis W. Aston. He was born at Camomile Green (not lawn) on the Harborne side of Smethwick. Mass spectrometry measures the mass to charge ratio of charged particles (I am still none the wiser).

It is said that Thomas Beebee, a locksmith of Bilston, invented the shoe buckle in 1686. However, Samuel Pepys wrote in his diary in 1660: 'This day I began to put on buckles to my shoes'.

On 18 November 1852, the date of the funeral of the Duke of Wellington, Mayor E.J. Creswell requested that the tradesmen of Dudley 'participating in the general national feeling, will testify their respect for the memory of that distinguished individual' by closing their shops. All the shops duly closed. I doubt it would happen today.

In Oldswinford a nailer, Joseph Orford, charged Thomas Barnes with being guilty of witchcraft, and boasted he would have him and his wife 'tuckt for witches'. This was in 1687, but the authorities dealt with Orford for being 'a common disturber' (of the peace).

Burial in a churchyard should be a solemn and dignified event and humour may not be appropriate. At St Johns in Kates Hill there were regular problems at the lower end of the churchyard with water seeping into open graves. Measures such as sawdust were used to minimise the effects of this. Locals often joked that: 'They doe actcherly bury 'em at St John's as launches 'em'.

Walsall Illuminations are second only to Blackpool in the league of autumn illuminations. They are held at Walsall

Arboretum. Built in 1874, it has been extended over the years and now covers over 80 acres, including a large boating lake. It was the site of the largest open limestone quarry in Walsall.

In 1845 the site was also the scene of a tragedy, when the Mayor of Walsall, John Harvey, drowned while swimming in flood water that had collected. Another man died during the rescue effort to save Harvey. It was thought by many that limestone-impregnated water was beneficial to health, but not on that day.

Black Country people have often been distrustful of banks. One supposedly true story is that of a young man who walked into a post office, with a reluctant old man following. The young man was carrying an old rusty tin.

The contents of the tin were handed over to be paid into a new savings account. There was over £1,000 in mildewed notes, stuck together because the tin had been buried in the garden for years. After the notes had been peeled apart and banked, the counter had to be disinfected.

There must have been something in the genes of Revd George Browne MacDonald, of Waterloo Road, Wolverhampton. His four daughters did rather well for themselves. Georgina married painter Sir Edward Burne-Jones, Louise was the mother of Stanley Baldwin MP, Agnes married painter Sir Edward John Poynter and Alice was mother to Rudyard Kipling.

Some of the world's oldest condoms were found during excavations at Dudley Castle. In the 1980s archaeological investigations were carried out there. The condoms were found in the lavatory (garderobe) of the keep, no doubt belonging to officers garrisoned in the castle during the English Civil War. They were reusable and probably intended to prevent disease rather than pregnancy.

St Mark's Church in Pensnett was known as the Cathedral of the Black Country. It was built in the 1840s.

29

DOING THE
NUMBERS

The number of Black Country towns with a Virgins End is
two: West Bromwich and Brierley Hill.

There are three Black Country footballers with memorials:
Billy Wright, Duncan Edwards, and Steve Bloomer.

During the Boer War, fifty-six Black Country men died; their
memorial is in Queens's Cross Cemetery, Dudley.

Between 1801 and 1901 in Darlaston, population increased
four-fold. In Willenhall it was six-fold and in Walsall it was
nine-fold.

In 1800 there were 160 collieries, with a total annual yield of
500,000 tons per annum.

By 1815 there were 200 collieries, with a total annual yield of
800,000 tons per annum.

By 1868 there were 540 collieries, with a total annual yield of
10,206,000 tons per annum.

In 1796 there were 14 blast furnaces by 1806 there were 42.

In 1829 the figure had risen to 123 and in 1868 there were
167, of which 80 were still in operation, though productivity
per furnace had improved.

In 1868 iron production ran at 855,000 tons of finished product from 2,100 puddling furnaces. It was claimed that the Black Country made half of Great Britain's finished iron. 20,000 people were employed in the Black Country iron trade, which had doubled in 68 years.

In 1868 400,000 locks were made each week in Wolverhampton and Willenhall, with 5,000 workers. 60,000 tons of chains and 5,000 tons of anchors were produced by 4,500 workers.

In 1801 there were only 29 saddlers and harness makers in Walsall. By 1841 the number had risen to 141. In 1901 employment peaked at 6,830 saddlers and harness makers, a quarter of the national total. By 1931 the decline in saddle making meant there were only 4,288 people employed in leather works, that figure was only 1730 in 1991. Even in the twenty-first century there are 90 leather companies in Walsall and over 70 saddlery manufacturers, the greatest concentration in the world.

By 1860, within five 5 miles of Dudley, there were:

44 pits
181 blast furnaces
118 iron works
79 rolling mills
1,500 puddling furnaces

No wonder the region was 'black'!

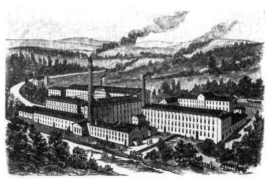

Still on the subject of miners, in a survey in the early nineteenth century the age and number of miners in one undisclosed area of the Black Country was noted by John Alfred Langford:

Aged	5 – 9	23
Aged	10 – 14	2,056
Aged	15 – 24	4,418
Aged	25 – 74	6,934
Aged	75+	129

When added together, the area covered by the thirty local authorities that covered the region in 1948 was 77,440 acres. In football pitch terms, a total of 44,251 football pitches would cover the whole area. Sunday morning footballer heaven!

30

BLACK COUNTRY AT WAR

In 1644, during the English Civil War, Parliamentary forces advanced towards Dudley Castle from Wednesbury. Two thousand Royalist troops were ordered to move to Dudley in response. As a result of this move the Parliamentary troops withdrew towards Tipton.

The Royalists saw this as an opportunity to attack the smaller force, and folklore has it that the battle took place at Tipton Green. The battle itself was inconclusive, with both sides suffering heavy casualties. It did, however, save the castle until 1646.

In 1855 two cannons were captured at Sebastopol during the Crimean War. These were installed near the Triple Gateway at Dudley Castle. In 1857 a 'joker' fired one of the cannon, which were spiked shortly afterwards to prevent a repeat performance.

The catchily named Metropolitan Carriage, Wagon and Finance Company Ltd, with a works at Oldbury, made many of the tanks used by the British Army during the First World War. It is said they actually made the first tank. By the end of the war over 2,600 tanks had been made in Britain.

The tank actually had its origins during the Crimean War, but the caterpillar track, essential for the 'landship' as it was first called, was conceived in 1770 by Richard Edgeworth. He described his invention as a 'cart which carried its own road'.

On 31 January 1916 there was a heavy air raid in the Black Country. Zeppelins homed in on the glow of the furnaces and attacked Tipton, Bradley, Wednesbury and Walsall; thirty-five people died in the raids. One was Julia Slater, Walsall's Lady Mayoress. Her tramcar was hit by bomb fragments and she died of septicaemia three weeks later.

In Tipton five members of the same family died when a bomb fell on their house in Union Street, and a courting couple died on the banks of the Wolverhampton Union Canal at Lower Bradley. Further raids took place in other areas of the Black Country around the same time; Halesowen and Cradley were both hit.

The Black Country was turned upside down with the advent of the Second World War: major buildings were painted to resemble fields, road blocks prepared for an invasion, barrage balloons flew overhead and smoke-generating equipment readied to create an even denser smoke pall in the event of air raids. These did not prevent bombing, after all it was an important strategic target for the Luftwaffe.

The first British man to die on D-Day in 1944 was born in Smethwick. He was Lieutenant Herbert Denham Brotheridge, who took part in the operation at Pegasus Bridge. His daughter Margaret was born just two weeks after his death. A memorial plaque to commemorate the events of his death was unveiled by Margaret at Smethwick Council House in 1995.

A Black Country man was one of the first to land in France on D-Day. On 6 June 1944 the first troops landed in Normandy as part of the D-Day landings. Early in the morning British Para troops landed and were greeted with a cheerful: 'Wear've yo bin – got 'ere wen yo cud?' from a very Black Country voice.

The 'meeter and greeter' was Netherton man Jack Palmer; one of a group of Signallers sent under cover of darkness to install cabling and communication equipment for the massive number of troops due to land, reclaim Europe and defeat Hitler.

On the morning of 5 June, Jack's unit were loaded onto a small fishing trawler with a variety of equipment. They crossed a mined beach and then headed across country towards Bayeux. The unit were told to expect 80 per cent casualties on this suicide mission. At 6 a.m. they watched as waves of allied Para troops dropped from the skies and fighters and bombers thundered overhead.

During the heat of battle they were surrounded by Germans and beat a hasty retreat. They took two further days to reach Bayeux. They then began work repairing overhead lines. Jack was wounded in the leg by a sniper, thankfully only a flesh wound, and he continued working, often operating in the face of stiff resistance.

Jack continued in his role as the allies broke out of Normandy. He advanced through Belgium and Germany and witnessed the terrifying events of the Battle of the Bulge.

A Brierley Hill Plane Crash in 1944 killed one person and caused extensive damage. On 16 March 1944 a Halifax bomber crashed on Adelaide Street in Brierley Hill. It had developed engine problems and the pilot and crew were forced to bail out.

More than sixty houses were damaged and the street blocked. Three Anderson shelters were uprooted and a gun turret was jammed into the kitchen of a house; four houses had to be demolished and others needed extensive repair. The crew escaped injury, but one woman sadly died. She had been staying with her parents, coincidentally whilst her husband was away serving in the RAF.

Bombing missions were very regular and accidents common. The wreckage of the Halifax was cleared away quickly and the houses repaired. The crash was reported briefly in local newspapers, and then the incident forgotten fairly quickly. The wreckage was dumped locally at Silver End, and children were soon salvaging souvenirs, including live tracer rounds. The police found where these rounds were located and recovered as many as they could.

Black Country generosity helped the war effort during the Second World War. The Battle of Britain was raging, mostly in the south of England, but Black Country towns played their part in the war effort. Money was raised to pay for a number of Spitfire fighters, the heroes of the Battle of Britain.

The *Express* and *Star* newspaper led the way; their readers raised £6,000 in six days to pay for 'The Inspirer' and inspire the Black Country it did! Other fighters were paid for by Black Country towns, one each for Halesowen, Rowley Regis, Wolverhampton, Smethwick, West Bromwich, Brierley Hill and Willenhall. Walsall raised enough money for two Spitfires.

Netherton firm Grazebrooks played an important role during the Second World War. They made the 8,000lb bombs, the first of which is said to have been dropped on the Gnome Works at Limoges in 1942, from a specially adapted Lancaster bomber.

The effect of two world wars was felt in ways we might not have considered. Some churches with churchyards, for example, saw the state of those sites deteriorate. One example was St John's at Kates Hill as a large number of the men from the area went to war, many not to return. Work was done between the wars to restore the neglect. Then came the Second World War and the pattern was repeated, except that after the war, no one took on the responsibility to restore the grounds, which again fell into disrepair.

All Saints Church in Darlaston was destroyed totally during the Second World War. The church in Walsall Street was the only one in the Lichfield diocese to be totally destroyed. On the 31 July 1942 it was hit by a bomb that should have landed on the nearby GKN factory.

TRAGEDY AND DISASTER

On 23 December 1844 eight miners descended into Corbyn's Hall Deep Pit. Something was heard to snap in the engine house and the chain carrying the skip ran freely. It took hours for a rescue team to descend using rope. They found the miners dead at the bottom of the shaft, submerged in the water of the sump at the bottom of the pit with the chain lying on top of them.

The oldest of those killed was aged 64 and the youngest, Job Brookes, was aged just 8. The majority were young boys. One miner had a lucky escape; Richard Leak tried to get into the skip, but it was full and he was told to go down on the next descent.

'The worst railway accident that has ever occurred in this country' happened in 1858 at Round Oak. Fourteen people died on an excursion train on its way back from Worcester. On the journey up the sharp incline between Brettell Lane and Round Oak, the train split in half, and the rear half careered back down the line. In the subsequent enquiry it was found that the guard did not apply the brake, because he was on the platform at Round Oak!

On 14 November 1872 Pelsall Hall Colliery was the site of a major mining disaster, where twenty-two men and boys died. Water broke into old mine workings with great force, trapping the miners underground. Only one cage of miners was able to escape in time. The rescue effort meant trying to remove the water and 60,000 gallons an hour were extracted. The operation lasted seven days and an estimated 6½ million gallons of water was removed. Eventually, twenty-one bodies were found, one miner, John Hubbard, was never found.

A terrible ironworks explosion on 2 July 1887 rocked Corngreaves Ironworks. A number of men were working at a blast furnace when a tuyere (a tube, nozzle or pipe through which air is blown into a furnace or hearth) exploded, hurling workmen in all directions.

Three men sustained shocking injuries and one was also badly scalded. The men were taken to the Dudley Guest Hospital but en route the man who had been scalded sadly died of his injuries.

This accident was unusual at the factory, which had a good safety record and no individual was at fault for the accident. The day after the incident another man died of his wounds. A few days later the coroner concluded that the death of the first man was 'accidental'.

A number of Black Country people perished on the ill-fated *Titanic* in April 1912. John Wesley Woodward was a cellist, born in West Bromwich. Three brothers and an uncle, also from West Bromwich, all died. James Lester was the uncle, Alfred, John Samuel and Joseph Davies made up the group. They were moving to Detroit to follow older members of the Davies family, who had already successfully settled there.

One of the most gruesome disasters in Black Country History happened in 1922 at Dudley Port. John Knowles started the Dudley Port Phosphor Bronze Company in 1916. In 1922 he bought 160 tons of cartridges, surplus from the First World War and planned to recover the lead bullet from its copper jacket. Knowles employed girls in their early teens, paying them 4s to 6s per week.

On 6 March, at a bout 11.45 a.m. a terrible blast shook Dudley Port. This was an explosion at Knowles' factory. A spark from an open fire had ignited the gunpowder discarded on the floor by the girls. The gunpowder was only occasionally swept up and deposited in the canal basin. Surely this was an accident waiting to happen.

Young girls ran wildly around the factory yard screaming. Some were stark naked, arms and legs scorched black, hair and eyebrows burnt. Despite the best efforts of hospital staff, nineteen girls died. The factory roof had been blown off and all the windows shattered; the walls were black and scarred. It is estimated that 30,000 people attended the funeral of twelve of the girls at Tipton Cemetery, where a vault was purchased by Tipton Council for a mass burial.

Knowles and his Works Manager, Chadwick, were charged. Knowles was sentenced to five years penal servitude. When asked why such young girls were carrying out the work, the reply was that it was not considered dangerous. A memorial was erected for the girls; it can still be seen in the cemetery.

A Dudley tragedy in 1934 shocked the region. During the Industrial Revolution the area around Dudley Castle was mined extensively for limestone which resulted in huge caverns. There were many openings and deep shafts that were dangerous to the unsuspecting explorer.

Saturday, 12 May 1934 was chosen by three youths for an exploration of the Castle grounds. One was 14-year-old Frederick Lester from Netherton; the other two boys were from Dudley. They made their way to the Tipton side of the grounds; then clambered to the top of Kettle Hill, where they were faced with a 150ft drop.

The boys climbed over the edge and began their descent. Half way down they lost their footing as the incline became steeper and they fell quickly to the bottom. Frederick plunged headlong into an obscured abyss. Employees at Castle Mill Works rushed to get to the hole, and the police were called. The rescue operation went on for many hours, and, as often happened when tragedy struck, hundreds of onlookers gathered.

By Tuesday there was still no sign of Frederick and the operation was suspended. Further attempts were made, but water levels had risen, hampering efforts yet again. The original entrance to the workings was found and officers crawled in, but they halted 30-40 yards later where the passage had either fallen in or been filled in. Tests also showed that the passage was about 60ft below the level of the water.

Finally, efforts were halted and three weeks after the tragedy, a sad funeral procession made its way to the air shaft where floral tributes were placed. The last rites were read and the sad party climbed the hill again and departed.

If you enjoyed this book, you may also be interested in…

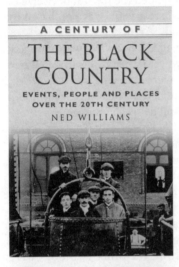

A Century of the Black Country

NED WILLIAMS

A Century of The Black Country offers an insight into the daily lives and living conditions of local people and gives the reader glimpses and details of familiar places during a century of unprecedented change. A striking account of the changes that have so altered the appearance of the region.

978 0 7509 4943 9

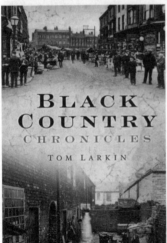

Black Country Chronicles

TOM LARKIN

Black Country Chronicles is a fascinating and multi-faceted narrative of twentieth-century life in the Black Country. Tom Larkin looks at the Black Country from the working-class point of view and records the significant contribution which these people made to the economic stability of the country as a whole.

978 0 7509 5084 8

Visit our website and discover thousands of other History Press books.

www.thehistorypress.co.uk

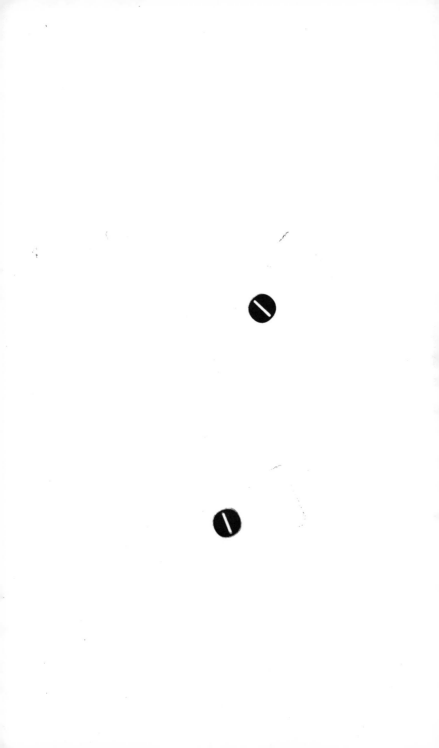